WHAT'S THAT MEAN?

by

DeLora Jenkins

Discussion Questions
by Roderick Huron

STANDARD PUBLISHING
Cincinnati, Ohio

2899

1971
STANDARD PUBLISHING
Cincinnati, Ohio
Printed in U.S.A.

CONTENTS

Chapter 1

Words—Words—Words

Lisa Stevens stood in puzzlement before the sandstone bluff that bore, like rich embroidery, the dark, unintelligible markings of Indian petroglyphs.

"What does this one mean?" she asked Dan Williams, pointing to a squiggly line moving in a large loop and intercepted by two bold black marks. "It looks almost like a trail, but it just goes in a loop."

Dan shook his head. "I can't tell you what that one means, but look at this one." He pointed to another drawing. "It's easy to see that this Indian is telling about a hunt. See the horns on the deer and the trail he's followed?"

"But in this one," Lisa went on, pointing stubbornly to the first drawing, "the artist surely could have made his meaning a little clearer." When Dan laughed she added, "If I were going to draw a picture to tell someone something, I wouldn't do such a poor job of it!"

"What about you and your shorthand?" Dan retorted. "It's not even easy for you to read what *you* draw!"

"What about *your* handwriting?" Lisa added laughingly.

"For that matter," the youth minister interrupted as he put a hand on each of their shoulders, "what about our words and everyday speech? How often do we say something and feel assured that the other person understands, only to learn later that he had no idea what we were really saying?"

"That's right," Dan replied. "Like the other night in youth meeting when I was trying to explain Romans 5:1. Ray told me later he hadn't the slightest idea what *justified* really meant, and I couldn't really explain it either."

"Somehow, it isn't easy to find words that suggest correct mental pictures," the youth minister agreed.

"We haven't progressed much, have we?" Lisa observed. "Indians drew pictures to say something; we say something to draw pictures." She pointed to the ambiguous petroglyph. "And neither of us are completely successful, are we?"

How much would we get out of a Biology class or Geometry class if we didn't understand the terms used in our textbooks? If we failed to master the basic concepts of genetics and photosynthesis, of isosceles triangles, parabolas, and trapezoids, we would not be likely to pass the courses. Indeed, it would be a terrible thing if we did pass, since we would be going on to more advanced courses still lacking the fundamental knowledge required.

Most of us have felt like ill-prepared students in an advanced course when we have picked up the Bible and tried to understand what we read. Because important terms and concepts mentioned in the Scriptures suggest no clear mental images for us, we read, and reread, then read again, and still do not understand.

6

We have probably shared Dan's confusion over the word *justified*. Looking at the verse he mentioned, Romans 5:1, we read: "Therefore being *justified* by faith—" The verb form *justified*, or the noun form *justification* are familiar expressions to the reader of the New Testament, but do we know what Paul meant when he used these terms in his letter to the Romans? What does it mean to us today?

Let us look at the word *sanctification*. There's a dusty word hidden on an unused shelf back in the corner of our minds. "For this is the will of God, even your *sanctification*—" (1 Thessalonians 4:3). Pretty important, isn't it? That is, if it is the will of God!

Take an easy word like *peace*. Who knows what it means? Hasn't it been a long time since anyone behaved as if he knew? What mental image does the following verse suggest: "Follow *peace* with all men—" (Hebrews 12:14)? With *all* men? That includes our enemies. Do we understand the concept?

Is there a *righteous* person alive? Don't we all tarnish a little at times? What pops into our minds when we hear this verse: "Except your *righteousness* shall exceed the *righteousness* of the scribes and Pharisees, ye shall in no case enter into the kingdom of heaven" (Matthew 5:20)? Jesus said these words in His great Sermon on the Mount. It is important for us to know what He is trying to teach us.

Singing the hymn, "That Old Time Religion," might make us clap our hands and tap our feet, but how do the words, "Makes me *love* everybody," affect us? If we have *love* problems, and the verse, "But I say unto you, *Love* your ene-

7

mies—" (Matthew 5:44), causes us to panic, maybe the concept of *love* is not clear in our minds.

Could we give a quick definition of Christian *sacrifice* in twenty-five words or less? How much help would the following verses provide: "By him therefore let us offer the *sacrifice* of praise . . . for with such *sacrifices* God is well pleased" (Hebrews 13:15, 16)?

Among the most familiar Bible terms are *faith* and *grace*. Do we understand them? Is *faith* believing in God? If so, why do we hear Christians say they wish they had more faith? Let us consider the phrase, "the *grace* of God." It is familiar to all Americans, from the statesmen and politicians to the drunk on skid row, but what happens when we try to explain *grace* to another person? Do we understand this verse: "That in the ages to come he might shew the exceeding riches of his *grace* in his kindness toward us through Christ Jesus" (Ephesians 2:7)?

Have any of us ever been accused of *judging*? We probably all have at some time. What is the Christian's approach to wrongdoing? Does he close his eyes, say nothing, think nothing, and feel nothing? Does he use the Bible to really "let 'em have it"? Does he see wrong and smooth it over? Perhaps we find it confusing that one passage of Scripture states, "*Judge* not, that ye be not *judged*," and another, "But he that is spiritual *judgeth* all things—" Without understanding important concepts including the concept of *judging*, it is easy to see why critics say that God's Word contradicts itself.

While considering controversial concepts, let's examine *predestination*. Has anyone ever stated to us that he was just not destined to be saved? Perhaps not, but how will we answer the question when someday someone does say it? And it is likely to happen! Will we state flatly that we do not understand what the term means and allow him to "convert" us to his definition?

Almost as archaic as *sanctification* is the term *covetousness*. Is it important? In Ephesians 5:5 it is listed with other sins of the highest magnitude: "For this ye know, that no whoremonger, nor unclean person, nor *covetous* man, who is an idolator, hath any inheritance in the kingdom of Christ and of God." Important? Not at all, unless we want to be heirs to the kingdom!

Fellowship is a word we all understand. It means fun, food, and well—*fellowship*! But does it? Let us consider Philippians 3:10: "That I may know him, and the power of his resurrection, and the *fellowship* of his sufferings—" Where is the fun and food in this verse? Evidently the word meant something else to Paul.

At this point we may feel we are facing a stone wall, so that we are to throw up our hands and say with Lisa: "He could surely have made his meaning a little clearer." Don't give up! Communication is difficult even for God, because He must use a human medium, words, to explain spiritual truths. Sometimes the mental pictures are distorted because human minds create them from the words. But God is not an imperfect man communicating with another imperfect man. His Word can be understood by less than perfect human beings and interpreted by His Holy Spirit as we read and study. James 1:5 gives us a joyful ray of hope in these words: "If any of you lack wisdom, let him ask of God, that giveth to all men

9

liberally, and upbraideth [scolds or reproaches] not; and it shall be given him."

So—let us get busy! Our God has promised us wisdom, and He is not an "Indian giver"!

Express Yourself

How good are you at communicating? Try this —pair off, then explain this statement to your partner: "In the beginning was the Word, and the Word was with God, and the Word was God." Have your partner give you an "instant replay" using his own words. Keep correcting him until he states to your satisfaction what you said when you explained it to him.

It's hard to get something across, isn't it?

Chapter 2

Contented, Not Covetous!

Kevin Holt shook beads of water from his face and ran his fingers through his dark hair. Hurry! Hurry! That was the word these days, especially between physical education and chemistry class. His eyes were so intent on the strands of hair he was endeavoring to comb in place that the sudden appearance of Bill Patterson's somber brown eyes in the mirror above him startled him. His momentary shock must have been evident because Bill grinned his wide grin that Dawson Tech girls raved about, especially Patti Johnson! *Lucky guy! With a face like yours around, how could I have a chance?* But there was a way—

Kevin let a smile work its way across his face. His eyes narrowed slightly. *OK, Bill, old man. Here's where the knife goes in.*

"Man, it's going to cost a bundle to take a girl to the banquet, isn't it?" he asked the face in the mirror. *Funny what a few words do. Your eyes are squinting at the corners. You can't hide your feelings from me.*

"Sure is!" Bill's voice sounded level enough. "Guess it's because the banquet is one of the biggest events on campus."

"Guess so," Kevin agreed.

Now turn it a little, Kev. "You're taking Patti, I suppose?" *Yessir, that hit home! No way at all. You won't be taking Patti anywhere!*

Kevin pushed his comb into a hip pocket and turned around to face Bill. Bill calmly continued to comb his hair. Nothing about his manner would tell most people that he was "shook," but Kevin knew he was! Bill Patterson didn't have a whisper of a chance of getting to the banquet, not with his uncle holding the purse strings. Since Bill's parents were killed he'd had to live with his uncle, John Patterson. Well, poor Bill never had a dime these days, although he worked every night and weekends at his uncle's store. He had one choice—stick it out until he graduated, or drop out of school. Bill had decided to stay in school.

"I'm not sure yet," Bill answered. He rinsed his comb under the faucet, tapped it gently against the sink, and put it into his pocket. Finally, his eyes met Kevin's. *Oh, yes, you are, Bill. You know you're not going. Too bad, fella. No money, no date!* Bill looked down at the floor. "You know I can't take Patti. Why ask?" Something in Bill's tone and manner told Kevin that Bill understood everything that he, Kevin, was thinking.

For just a minute Kevin almost wavered. There had been a day when he and Bill were pretty good friends, before he wanted things so much, and especially before Patti. *If I didn't want your girl, I could help you, but I do want her. Without you in the picture, I'll have a chance.*

"Well, I know who I'm asking," Kevin said. *And so do you!* He pushed his way through the heavy door into the bright sunlight. Was it his fault that he knew how to raise twenty bucks in time for the banquet? He'd be a fool to tell Bill how to earn it, wouldn't he?

12

That's right, Bill. I want the money. And I plan to have Patti Johnson, if I have to walk all over you to get her!

Let's consider the concept of *covetousness*. Does *covetousness* sound like a term out of the Dark Ages? Well, it is. Actually, it goes even farther back in history than that. It goes back to the day Satan tempted Eve and she coveted the forbidden fruit of the tree of knowledge of good and evil. But let us not think that *covetousness* is limited to the past. It extends right up to this very day, to this minute, and to each of us.

"Me?" Some of us may think. "*Covetousness*? I don't know how to spell the word, or even pronounce it. For that matter, what *is* it?"

Spelling and pronunciation are minor problems, but *covetousness* is a major problem that must be solved, if it involves the "now generation." *Webster's New World Dictionary* gives this modern definition of the word *covet*: "To desire earnestly (especially something another person has), crave, long for. Synonym: envy." Let us compare this modern definition with the New Testament Greek meaning of the word *pleonexia*, translated *covetousness*. *Pleonexia* is the characteristic of a person who is always ready to sacrifice someone else to gain something for himself. It is defined in *Young's Analytical Concordance of the Bible* as "the wish to have more." Apparently there has been little change in the meaning over the years.

Are we suddenly seeing the picture? "Willing to sacrifice anything or anyone else to gain something for himself." It is not hard to focus Kevin Holt into this scene, is it? Can you think of

13

people who always try to "keep up with the Joneses," even though they cannot afford it? Can you think of someone you know who seems to need the same things—clothes, cars, what have you—that "all his friends" have, no matter what it may cost his parents? Can we recognize ourselves in the scene?

Well, what is wrong with getting what we want out of life? If Kevin gets that date with Patti, what's so wrong about that? After all, it's everyone for himself in this world, isn't it?

First, let us establish whether or not Kevin was *covetous*. Was he willing to sacrifice someone else to gain something for himself? What was his last mental statement? "And I plan to have Patti Johnson, *if I have to walk all over you to get her*!" Was he covetous? What was wrong with wanting a date with Patti, or trying to get that date? Nothing! What about plotting to get her away from Bill? This is where *covetousness* comes into the picture. He was willing to sacrifice Bill to gain something for himself. That is *covetousness*.

What causes *covetousness*? The apostle Paul mentions a cause of *covetousness* as he writes to the church at Rome: "And even as they did not like to retain God in their knowledge, God gave them over to a reprobate [depraved or vicious] mind, to do those things which are not convenient; being filled with all unrighteousness, fornication, wickedness, *covetousness*" (Romans 1:28, 29).

"They did not like to retain God in their knowledge." They chose to ignore God. Outside of God, and by the standards of the world, Kevin was clever; but, if Kevin were a Christian, the

14

picture would change. He would be ignoring God's command to love his neighbor as himself. He would be ignoring God, for God is love. Further, Kevin would be committing a sin, for, as Paul states, "For this ye know, that no whoremonger, nor unclean person, nor *covetous* man, who is an idolator, hath any inheritance in the kingdom of Christ and of God" (Ephesians 5:5).

Well, where does *covetousness* begin? We should know this because it is more difficult to fight sin once it has taken hold in our life. Jesus himself gives us this answer: "From within, out of the heart of men, proceed evil thoughts, adulteries, fornications, murders, thefts, *covetousness*, wickedness, deceit, lasciviousness, an evil eye, blasphemy, pride, foolishness: all these evil things come from within, and defile the man" (Mark 7:21-23). Covetousness begins in the heart. Man thinks about what he wants, and he doesn't stop himself from thinking and planning wrongfully to get what he wants. This defiles (makes unclean) the man. Is this what Kevin did? Ignoring God and thus drawn away from God by his own desire, which James calls "lust" (James 1:14), he was all for taking Bill's girl however he could. Thus he became *covetous*.

What is so wrong with covetousness? What results come from it? Again, God's Word does not leave us uninformed: "Mortify [put to death] therefore your members which are upon the earth [do not live with the following things in your life]; fornication, uncleanness, inordinate affection, evil concupiscence [misused sexual desires], and *covetousness,* which is idolatry: for which things' sake the wrath of God cometh on the children of disobedience" (Colossians 3:5, 6).

15

Notice that Paul labels the covetous man an idolator and covetousness idolatry.

What was the main cause of the downfall of Israel, the nation God called out of Egypt to be His own? It was idolatry. What was the burden of the pleas and the warnings of all the prophets? To turn from idols and serve the living God. Instead of quoting numerous passages from the Old Testament, let us consider Stephen's brief account: "And they made a calf in those days, and offered sacrifice unto the idol, and rejoiced in the works of their own hands. Then God turned, and gave them up to worship the host of heaven; as it is written in the book of the prophets, O ye house of Israel, have ye offered to me slain beasts and sacrifices by the space of forty years in the wilderness? Yea, ye took up the tabernacle of Moloch, and the star of your god Remphan, figures which ye made to worship them: and I will carry you away beyond Babylon" (Acts 7:41-43).

Two things should be evident from these Scripture verses. First, *covetousness* is always listed in the Bible with sins of a very wicked nature: adultery, misused sexual drives, murder, wickedness, thefts, pride, and blasphemy. Second, God's wrath will come upon the disobedient man who chooses to continue in this sin.

Just for a challenge, each of us should read some of these instances of *covetousness* cited in God's Word: Ananias and Sapphira (Acts 5:1-11) who coveted the glory of men for giving money to the church, and lied to receive that glory; the rich farmer (Luke 12:16-21) who had more than enough for himself but coveted it all for himself; the man named Simon who tried to buy the power to give the Holy Spirit to others

16

by the laying on of hands (Acts 8:19). Read also the result in each case. Covetousness, which Paul labels idolatry, turns the mind and heart away from God. "Where your treasure [whatever you earnestly strive for] is, there will your heart be also" (Matthew 6:21). God, the Creator, who alone is to be worshiped, absolutely will not be dethroned.

The Christian strives to keep himself from covetousness. There's a good social application here as well as the Christian application. How many of us would want a friend like Kevin, an employer with his characteristics, or a spouse with his characteristics?

What is God's answer to *covetousness*?

"But godliness with contentment is great gain. For we brought nothing into this world, and it is certain we can carry nothing out. And having food and raiment let us be therewith content" (1 Timothy 6:6-8).

There's a big "C" in Christian, and it stands for Contented, not Covetous!

Express Yourself

Defend one of these viewpoints: (1) The American way is to "get all you can, can all you get, and sit on the can"; or (2) Americans are the most generous and unselfish people in the world.

Is there something about wanting money and things that is detrimental to Christian growth? Is wanting money evil in itself? Is money itself evil? Should a Christian ever want to become rich?

17

Chapter 3

Except for the Grace of God

Jerry Crawley watched the unkempt man walk into the local bar. The man's neck was settled deeply into his shoulders and he walked with a strangely defeated gait. Both of his hands were shoved deep into baggy pants pockets. In this dejected state, Ed Minton seemed an old man.

"I can't help feeling sorry for him," Jerry said to his friends who were walking with him.

"Sorry for old Ed Minton? You must be crazy, Jerry!" chided a snub-nosed young man known as Chub. "Look at him. It's barely ten in the morning, and there he goes into the bar to start another day."

"Things have gone badly for Ed," Jerry answered.

"That's right," agreed dark-haired Carlos. "I heard that he used to be quite a wheel around town before Johnson wiped him out and took over his business."

Chub ran a pudgy hand over his head. He was so irritated that Jerry would not have been surprised to see sparks flying from the bristles of his red hair.

"So that gives him an excuse, huh? The first time trouble strikes, old Ed Minton hits the bottle. Look at my dad. He didn't end up an old sot!"

Jerry nodded. Chub had a right to be proud of his father. He had lost both legs during World War II and then had come home to a wife dying of cancer. Today he was a successful commercial lawyer.

"But we don't know all the facts about Ed," Carlos argued.

"It depends on the man," Chub continued stubbornly. "The way I see it, you get what you earn in life. And what's he earning for himself by boozing it up? Self-respect? A day's wages?" Chub shook his head. "All he has earned himself is a hangover."

Still arguing, Carlos asked, "What about Edwin Finch, Chub? What did he ever do to earn the fifty grand Granny Finch left him? I wouldn't call him an example of a great guy."

"Carlos has a point there," Jerry agreed. "Finch has hurt more small businessmen in this town than any other man I know. Yet he's added Granny Finch's real estate to his assets. Did he deserve anything?"

"Say what you want to," Chub answered, plainly disturbed by the truth of these statements. "Old Ed is still just a drunk, and I can't feel too sorry for him."

"And Edwin Finch is an old swindler who didn't deserve Granny Finch's homestead," Carlos added.

"Oh, I don't agree that Ed's way of life is right," Jerry said. "It's just that I feel sorry that he's like he is. Dirty, ragged clothes, and half drunk all the time. It's true he's earned nothing but disrespect, Chub, but I'd feel sorry for any man who lives as he does, and especially when no one cares that he lives that way."

20

Jerry thought a while and then concluded the conversation. "As a matter of fact," he admitted, "I get lots of things I don't deserve either. How about you, Chub? Don't you think you should consider that?" Jerry raised a hand in salute and started up the walk that led to his house, leaving his friends in silent contemplation.

Most of us have heard someone "say grace" at the table, and as we focus on these words, our mental eye envisions people around a dining table with heads bowed in prayer. We all have heard or read a statement similar to this: "She has so much grace." This expression brings forth the mental picture of a girl who is anything but awkward or clumsy. But what do we see mentally when we hear the words, "God's grace" or "the grace of God"? Do these expressions draw any clear picture in our minds? If not, that is not very surprising. The concept of *grace* is "as big as God" and as difficult for us to understand. But let us sort out what the Scripture says about *grace* in order to form a picture in our minds. It may take the rest of our lives to fill in the rough sketch we draw today, but we can begin now to "see" *grace*.

It is not hard to understand that we all sin. All of us have done sinful things we are ashamed of, and God knows each of those things. But what God does about those sins is hard for us to understand because it is so different from what we would do if we were God. The concept of God's *grace* is described by the apostle Paul: "And you hath he quickened, who were dead in trespasses and sins; wherein in time past ye walked according to the course of this world, according to the

21

prince of the power of the air [Satan], the spirit that now worketh in the children of disobedience: among whom also we all had our conversation [manner of life] in times past in the lusts of our flesh, fulfilling the desires of the flesh and of the mind; and were by nature the children of wrath, even as others. But God, who is rich in mercy, for his great love wherewith he loved us, even when we were dead in sins, hath quickened us together with Christ, (by *grace* ye are saved;) and hath raised us up together, and made us sit together in heavenly places in Christ Jesus: that in the ages to come he might shew the exceeding riches of his *grace* in his kindness toward us through Christ Jesus" (Ephesians 2:1-7).

God doesn't think the way we do. While we say with Chub, "You get what you earn in life," God says, "You are freely offered a gift that you did not earn." To be exact, the Bible says, "For the wages of sin is death [and we have all sinned]; but the gift of God is eternal life through Jesus Christ our Lord" (Romans 6:23). God looks at us and sees us in our sinful state looking much like "old Ed Minton." But somewhat as Jerry saw the same man, God is "sorry for any man who lives as he does." Unlike either of the boys, however, God goes beyond sympathy. While man deserves or earns nothing but death, God cares and has made it possible for man to attain eternal life. Even before we knew about God, before we were ever born, God extended His *grace* to us. *Grace* provides an unearned gift of forgiveness of sins and eternal life to the believer. The sinner who is worthy of death is given life instead, through the gift of God's Son.

Now, some of us may be tempted to think,

"That's wonderful of God to provide this fine gift, but what kind of man would take it without trying to do something to earn it?" This idea is not new. Most human beings are proud. Like Chub, we have learned from society that to retain our self-respect we must earn whatever we receive. We must put aside this idea when we consider our relationship with God. There is no way of earning *grace*. We are wholly dependent on God for it. The Christians in Galatia were falling prey to the idea that by keeping the law of Moses they could earn salvation in Christ. Paul wrote them a letter with these words: "I do not frustrate the *grace* of God: for if righteousness come by the law, then Christ is dead in vain" (Galatians 2:21). The well-meaning Galatians could not earn salvation. But some similar notions exist today. We have all heard: "Maybe I'm not a Christian, but I'm a good citizen, and do good in the community, and live by the golden rule." People who say these things seem to believe that they deserve salvation as a reward for doing good. The fact remains that the good moral man cannot earn salvation; it comes only through the grace of God. Even then, the person must accept Christ through whom the gift is given.

There is no end to grace. Accepting Christ as our Saviour only begins the process of grace in the life of the believer. One important blessing it provides is continual forgiveness of sin. "If we confess our sins, he is faithful and just to forgive us our sins, and to cleanse us from all unrighteousness" (1 John 1:9).

Grace calls believers to be used of God in teaching, preaching, singing, and otherwise serving Him. It also equips the believer with the power of God to perform that service. This truth is set forth in Ephesians 3:7-9: "Whereof I [Paul] was made a minister, according to the gift of the *grace* of God given unto me by the effectual working of his power. Unto me, who am less than the least of all saints, is this *grace* given, that I should preach among the Gentiles the unsearchable riches of Christ; and to make all men see [by the power of God] what is the fellowship of the mystery, which from the beginning of the world hath been hid in God, who created all things by Jesus Christ."

And Paul continues the same thought in 1 Corinthians 15:10: "But by the *grace* of God I am what I am: and his *grace* which was bestowed upon me was not in vain; but I laboured more abundantly than they all [other apostles—see v. 9]: yet not I, but the *grace* of God [the power] which was with me."

Peter states that Christians must use the grace of God as good stewards, "As every man hath received the gift, even so minister the same one to another, as good stewards of the manifold *grace* of God. If any man speak, let him speak as the oracles of God; if any man minister, let him do it as of the ability which God giveth . . ." (1 Peter 4:10, 11).

The *grace* God has given to us is communicated to others through us. The gifts of material things given by the churches of Macedonia to the needy Christians in Jerusalem was described as *grace* by Paul in 2 Corinthians 8.

We do not fully understand *grace*, but we know something about it:

Grace is expressed in the gift to man of salvation, through Jesus Christ's atoning sacrifice.

Grace extends accessible forgiveness for a life-time.

Grace is given in man's call to serve God.

Grace causes the believers to love one another and provide for the needs of those less fortunate.

We have seen what grace *accomplishes*, but what *is* it? Perhaps it is best defined in these Scriptures:

"But God commendeth his love toward us, in that, while we were yet sinners, Christ died for us" (Romans 5:8).

"By this shall all men know that ye are my disciples, if ye have love one to another" (John 13:35).

These passages help us to see that a man like Ed Minton, or even worse, is within the reach of God's grace. That grace can be extended to him through the understanding, patience, and love of someone like Jerry, who gives evidence of the presence of God's grace at work in his heart. Is that grace active in us?

Express Yourself

Is it true that God will save us only if we do our best all the time and always remember to pray for forgiveness for each sin we commit? What would happen if we were to die with sins on our record for which we had neglected to ask forgiveness?

Do you think God's grace is so great that He will save everyone in the world? Do you think that those who consider baptism a requirement for salvation may be frustrating God's grace?

Chapter 4

Faith Is Fact

Steve Brunner looked thoughtfully at the dazzling white buildings hugging the ground. It was a fitting design for the ultramodern laboratory it housed. Steve's Freshman Science Club was touring the lab to examine the field of radiology firsthand. As they walked through the tinted glass foyer into the shadowed corridors, excitement grew in Steve. It was almost like stepping into the future. Electronic equipment chattered out data onto cards. Tapes with incessant regularity in the sound gave the lab an atmosphere of excited activity.

"There you are. Right on time!" The voice belonged to a tall young technician in a white lab coat. "Dr. Mason selected me as your tour guide." He shook hands with Steve's instructor. "You must be Professor Swanson." Turning back to the students he introduced himself as Larry Dodds, a physical science technician.

In the X-ray Analysis Lab, the class was introduced to X-ray fluorescence as they watched soil samples being analyzed. Long rolls of graph paper unwound in constant movement as the fine etching drew evidence of the unseen elements.

In the Liquid Scintillation Lab, the technician walked up to a piece of equipment that looked much like a dishwasher from a distance. He lifted the top and exposed the interior. Steve looked around for a light switch in the room. The room was not well lighted.

"Do you always work in the dark?" someone asked.

"Semidarkness," the technician replied. "This method determines radiation activity by the measuring of light of the gamma rays. We're counting tritium in this scintillator." Pointing to several capped vials he continued, "Samples of tritium, or radioactive hydrogen, are put into these vials in a 'cocktail,' that is, an organic mixture, to speed up scintillation. The photoelectric cell in the well crystal converts the scintillations, or light flashes, from the radioactive material into signals which can be measured."

As Steve looked around the room, he was fascinated by the silent discernible activity present in the red numbers being flashed electronically on screens, and the meters registering electrical charges. Everything in the laboratory seemed to be capturing movement and recording the data with unbelievable speed.

"It's amazing how something so powerful as a gamma ray can be invisible," one student observed.

"But you can see it," Steve insisted. "At least you can see what it does. What about the etchings on the graph paper, or the computer tapes, or the flashing numbers on the electronic screens—"

"And in the effects upon living substance, or living organisms," the technician added. "We can never allow ourselves to minimize the effects of radiation upon life itself, good effects as well as the bad effects. That is why I'm here working in this laboratory."

28

Linda looked wide-eyed at the "Caution—Radiation Hazard" sign on a closed door. "Are we getting any radiation right now?"

"No more than you would anywhere else," the technician assured her. He grinned broadly. "You've been living with radiation all your life, young lady."

"But I've never been so aware of it before!" she exclaimed.

"It's good that you are aware of it," the technician said, "Radioactive energy is the most powerful scientific force in the world today."

Atomic energy has always been available to man, but man took a long time to discover it. Much like the subject of atomic power, *faith* with all its power has always been available to man, but he must discover it. God's Word is the source for *faith*. We know this because the apostle Paul said: "So then *faith* cometh by hearing, and hearing by the word of God" (Romans 10:17).

Consider *faith*. What is it? How can we tell if we have it? Suppose you decide to ask five Christians and five non-Christians what the word *faith* means; or, suppose you were to ask ten people from ten different congregations the same question. What would they answer? Actually, you would probably receive about twenty different answers. Many people do not understand what *faith* is, and yet God's Word tells us, "Without *faith* it is impossible to please him" (Hebrews 11:6). Perhaps the most commonly stated definition of *faith* is "believing in God." Do you agree that this is *faith*? If you do, you may be surprised to learn that James, the New Testament writer, did not consider this definition entirely sufficient

29

for the Christian. He writes: "Thou believest that there is one God; thou doest well: the devils also believe, and tremble" (James 2:19).

Yes, many people believe and tremble and do nothing further. James implies that the Christian must do more. Well, since *faith* is more than belief that there is a God, what else is it? Much of the New Testament deals with the concept of *faith*, but no one chapter speaks so vividly on the subject as does Hebrews 11. It is in this "faith chapter" that we find this definition of *faith*: "Now *faith* is the substance of things hoped for, the evidence of things not seen" (Hebrews 11:1). That is the definition of the unseen quality of *faith*. After this summary statement, the author of Hebrews begins at the beginning to draw a visible picture of that invisible force, *faith*.

"Through *faith* we understand that the worlds were framed by the word of God, so that things which are seen were not made of things which do appear" (v. 3). Is there a similarity in this thought and that of the atomic structure of the world we see? "Things which are seen . . . made of things not seen." This verse also tells us that *faith* makes it possible to understand Genesis 1:1: "In the beginning God created the heaven and the earth."

It took men many years to discover the atom because it could not be seen, but, as the technician told Linda in the story we just read, the energy of the atom can produce devastatingly visible changes in animal and plant life. Like the energy of the atom, *faith* is an invisible force that causes visible effects. Unlike atomic energy, which can be used for good or evil effects, however, the Christian's faith always brings about good effects.

30

Faith is a motivation for action. Shall we prove this statement? Below in elliptic form are verses from Hebrews 11. Take a pencil and a piece of paper and examine the underlined words in this text. At the top of the page make headings for two lists labeling one NOUN or PRONOUN, the other VERB. Now, from the underlined words select the proper list and write the words under that heading. (The complete verses should be read from the Bible in order for you to get the entire thought content, but the elliptic form is used here for brevity.)

"By faith *Abel offered* unto God a more excellent sacrifice . . ." (v. 4).

"By faith *Enoch* . . . that he *pleased* God. But without faith it is impossible to please him . . ." (vv. 5, 6).

"By faith *Noah* . . . *prepared* an ark" (v. 7).

"By faith *Abraham* . . . *obeyed*; and he went out . . ." (v. 8).

"By faith *he sojourned* . . ." (v. 9).

"By faith *Abraham*, when he was tried, *offered* Isaac . . ." (v. 17).

"By faith *Isaac* . . . *blessed* Jacob and Esau concerning things to come" (v. 20).

"By faith *Jacob* . . . *blessed* both the sons of Joseph; and *worshipped*, leaning upon the top of his staff" (v. 21).

"By faith *Moses*, when he was born, *was hid* three months of his parents . . ." (v. 23). (The parents' faith is demonstrated in this instance.)

"By faith *Moses* . . . *refused* to be called the son of Pharaoh's daughter; *choosing* rather *to suffer affliction* with the people of God, than to enjoy the pleasures of sin for a season" (vv. 24, 25).

"By faith he [*Moses*] *forsook* Egypt, not fearing the wrath of the king; for *he endured*, as seeing him who is invisible" (v. 27).

"Through faith he [*Moses*] *kept the passover*, and the sprinkling of blood, lest he that destroyed the firstborn should touch them" (v. 28).

"By faith they [*Israel*] *passed through* the Red sea as by dry land . . ." (v. 29).

"By faith the *walls of Jericho fell down*, after they were compassed about seven days" (v. 30). (In this instance, the Israelites exercised faith.)

"What shall I more say? For the time would fail me to tell of *Gedeon*, and of *Barak*, and of *Samson*, and of *Jephthae*; of *David* also, and *Samuel*, and of the *prophets*: who through faith *subdued* kingdoms, *wrought* righteousness, *obtained* promises, *stopped* the mouths of lions, *quenched* the violence of fire, *escaped* the edge of the sword, out of weakness *were made strong*, *waxed valiant* in fight, *turned to flight* the armies of the aliens" (vv. 32-34).

Examining the lists of these underlined words, we can see that there are many verbs, and verbs denote action. Can you mentally see an electronic counter machine flashing out data on the activity of one of these samples? Can you imagine Noah as the sample, faith as the activity present in the sample, and the ark as the data being recorded? In none of these verses did we find *faith* without *action*; faith is always the motivation for action. If the first step in the concept of *faith* is belief in God, then what is the second step? By examining your own lists you can soon determine that the continuing step of faith is acting on that belief.

It is true, as Steve recognized, that the alpha, beta, and gamma rays of radioactive materials can be seen through their effects on living objects, and the activity of these materials can be measured on counting and recording equipment. In the same way *faith* can be seen in the world by its effect upon the lives of men, and can be measured by the actions it produces. That great giant, atomic energy, will someday power factories, light our homes, change sea water into drinking water, run engines, and cook our food. But the power of *faith* is even greater. Faith will cause men to sit with Christ in heavenly places through the resurrection from the dead.

Through *faith*, Paul completed three missionary journeys; through *faith* Peter went to the house of Cornelius; through *faith* the early church went everywhere preaching the gospel. Through *faith* men today enter the ministry, do evangelistic calling, go to the mission fields, build churches and Bible colleges, live sanctified lives that witness for Christ, and watch for the second coming of our Lord. Through *faith* the campus Christian endures the scorn and ridicule of nonbelieving classmates. Through *faith* he takes a stand for his belief, in the face of liberal religious teaching. Through *faith* he seeks to help his peers find some answers to their problems instead of escapism in drugs.

You may be able to add to the list of men and women in the faith chapter those people you've known personally who acted on their faith. If you are a Christian, you can add yourself to the list also, because you will always be a cause for action for Christ. You'll have a *faith* that is alive and not dead; *faith* that pleases God; *faith* that is the motivating force for the things you do. You will study God's Word and absorb daily portions of His irradiating energy. You will "Go . . . into all the world, and preach the gospel"; "pray without ceasing"; "love your neighbour"; and "walk by faith." Your *faith* can be seen, because it will cause you to "Let your light so shine before men, that they may see your good works, and glorify your Father which is in heaven" (Matthew 5:16).

Express Yourself

What do you think of when someone says, "You just have to accept it by faith, that's all"? Should we be content to accept the Bible by faith, or should we look for evidences to support the Biblical record?

What is the difference between believing in God and believing in Santa Claus?

Analyze this statement: Faith is what you do, not what you believe.

Chapter 5

Judging:
Evaluation or Condemnation?

Gary Johnson walked defiantly out onto the campus lawn, pulled the pack of cigarettes from his shirt pocket, and stood there trying to look casual. Several times that morning he had seen the surprised looks on the faces of the other seminary class members. All except Joy's—she had looked a little sick. Mr. Peterson, the teacher, hadn't seemed to notice at all. But he had, because every time his eyes lifted from his lesson material they seemed to fasten on the bulge of Gary's pocket. Gary could almost hear sentence being passed on him.

Standing there on the lawn he watched the professor talking with Joy. Gary's hand trembled ever so slightly as he lit the cigarette. Drawing deeply, he sent a stream of smoke curling through the people visiting in little groups around him.

I wonder if she'll speak? he mused. *She'll probably just walk away.* Ron and Mary walked by him. Just as well. They had never known he was alive before, why start now? Mr. Peterson came through the crowd with outstretched hand, looking him right in the eye. Gary held the cigarette behind him and shook the offered hand.

"Good morning, Gary!" There was a hesitation. "I'd like to drop by your dorm Thursday evening, if I may."

"OK, Mr. Peterson. I'll be there." *Well! It's coming. I'll probably get the old third degree Thursday night.* Gary grinned. He would be ready with Mr. Peterson's own little crutch, the Scriptures! "Judge not, that ye be not judged." That's all he would say. There was no answer to that.

What Gary Johnson planned to say to Mr. Peterson probably sounds familiar to all of us. Haven't we all heard someone say nearly those same words to us at some time? It may not always be a direct quote, but who hasn't heard someone say, "What right does he have to *judge* me?" We constantly hear of the new morality, nonconformity, the increasing use of drugs. "Who can say that all the people who do these things are wrong?" some people ask. "Maybe they are right and you are wrong." Any person may hear these words occasionally, but no one hears them more often than the Christian. Society accuses him, "You set yourself up as a *judge*, and you have no right to *judge!*"

What about *judging*? As Christians should we *judge*? If so, what or whom can we *judge*, and by what standards? Let us look more closely into this matter.

The apostle Paul said that he had judged a man: "For I verily, as absent in body, but present in spirit, have judged already, as though I were present, concerning him that hath so done this deed" (1 Corinthians 5:3). Without even being present, Paul had *judged* a man's deeds. Was he wrong in doing this? Why did he *judge* the man, and how did he *judge* him? We'll need some background for this incident in order to answer these questions.

Paul was telling the church people at Corinth that they were doing wrong because they had a member who was having sexual relations (fornication) with his father's wife (talk about "new" morality!) He begins with these words: "It is reported commonly that there is fornication among you, and such fornication as is not so much as named among the Gentiles, that one should have his father's wife" (1 Corinthians 5:1). Paul was *judging* the act itself. That it involved a man and his father's wife only made the act more distasteful. What can we *judge*? We can *judge*, that is, recognize or determine, certain acts as ungodly. Paul was familiar with the Commandment, "Thou shalt not commit adultery," and with Jesus' words, "But I say unto you, That whosoever looketh on a woman to lust after her hath committed adultery with her already in his heart" (Matthew 5:28). Paul was using the standard of God's Word to *judge* the act. Whom did he judge? He hurries to tell the church that they should withdraw themselves from that church member: "But now I have written unto you not to keep company, if any man that is called a brother be a fornicator, or covetous, or an idolator, or a railer, or a drunkard, or an extortioner; with such an one no not to eat. For what have I to do to *judge* them also that are without? Do not ye *judge* them that are within?" (1 Corinthians 5:11, 12). This is a pretty severe judgment. It was a judgment upon the behavior of a man who was known openly as a gross fornicator. He was committing acts that were not even "named among the Gentiles." For the good of the church in Corinth and as a wit-

37

ness to the unbelievers, the members were to withdraw themselves from that man's company.

Some may protest that this was Paul the apostle, and we are just ordinary persons. Can "ordinary" Christians *judge*? Paul answered this question when he said, "But the natural man receiveth not the things of the Spirit of God: for they are foolishness unto him: neither can he know them, because they are spiritually discerned. But he that is spiritual *judgeth* all things, yet he himself is *judged* of no man" (1 Corinthians 2:14, 15). Paul also tells us that we Christians should *judge* ourselves when we partake of the Lord's Supper: "But let a man examine himself, and so let him eat of that bread, and drink of that cup. For if we would *judge* ourselves, we should not be judged. But when we are judged, we are chastened of the Lord, that we should not be condemned with the world" (1 Corinthians 11:28, 31, 32).

Thus it is clear that Christians should *judge*, in the sense of evaluating evidence (words or acts) by God's Word and making a decision. We must harmonize this truth, however, with Jesus' familiar words: "*Judge* not, that ye be not *judged*. For with what *judgment* ye *judge*, ye shall be *judged*: and with what measure ye mete, it shall be measured to you again" (Matthew 7:1, 2).

Is there a contradiction? Not at all. The Scriptural concept of judging has two sides. We've already examined one, that of reaching a decision after evaluating the evidence by the standard of God's Word. There is another side, that of passing sentence on that decision, or condemning. When Jesus said, "Judge not, that ye be not judged,"

38

He meant, "Do not condemn, or you will be in danger of being condemned." Why did He say this? Paul's words to the church at Corinth provide a good answer: "For what have I to do to judge them also that are without? But them that are without God *judgeth*" (1 Corinthians 5:12, 13). And of the Romans he asks, "Who art thou that *judgest* another man's servant? to his own master he standeth or falleth . . . But why dost thou judge thy brother? or why dost thou set at nought thy brother? for we shall all stand before the judgment seat of Christ" (Romans 14:4, 10).

In the case of the church withdrawing from the man, it was an act of rebuke by the Christians. It was not intended to condemn the man, but to bring him to repentance.

We usurp God's authority when we condemn another person. One side of the Scriptural concept of judging belongs to us—evaluation and decision; the other side belongs to God, who only has the authority to pronounce the sentence of condemnation or salvation.

Express Yourself

Is there any difference, and if so, what, between "Let everyone do his own thing," and "Judge not, that ye be not judged"? Is it any of our business as Christians to say anything to people we know who are doing wrong?

Can a person still be a Christian and smoke? Use profanity? Sniff glue? Smoke pot? Mainline heroin? Push LSD? What about watching TV and movies? Where would you draw the line, if at all?

Chapter 6

Just-As-If-I'd Never

Todd's eyes wavered under the piercing look of Judge Nelson.

"Did you have the watch in your possession, Todd?" Judge Nelson questioned. His heavy eyebrows overhanging sober brown eyes gave Todd the feeling that he was facing God.

Silence was alive in the room as the judge waited. In the pit of Todd's stomach a warmth grew that made him feel he would lose his breakfast right there in the judge's chambers. His eyes shifted to either side, but Mom and Dad sat there in silence. He must answer for himself.

"Yes, Sir," he answered, while his mind echoed the words, "I am guilty!"

"Did you know, Son?" Dad's voice was thick with emotion.

"Not absolutely, Dad. But I did have a feeling about it. When Jim handed me the watch and asked me to put it into the glove compartment of my car, I should have known."

Turning to the judge, Todd spoke quietly, "Sir, I did have the watch, and because I wanted to help Jim, I am guilty."

Mom began to cry softly. Dad put his hand on Todd's shoulder. Todd closed his eyes and drew in a deep breath, waiting for the judge's sentence.

"Todd, it is true that having the watch in your possession makes you an accessory, and therefore guilty. But, because this is your first offense and you have obviously been given fine family training, your offense will not be recorded against you this time."

Todd's mouth twisted crazily. "You mean— You mean, Sir, that it's just as if I'd never been involved?"

"That's right," the judge answered. "You're free of any charge, just as though you'd never been involved. But from now on, young man, you must guard your freedom more carefully by right actions."

Have you ever been in trouble with the law? Probably not. Have you ever been in trouble to a lesser degree than that? Actually, all of us are "in trouble" when we face the holiness of God and find ourselves in desperate need.

God's Word uses a word with big meaning to explain the answer to our need when we face God's holiness: *justified*. While this is a word requiring deep and sober thought, it is possible to understand it. Words are only a means of drawing mental pictures. Keep in mind Todd's story as you read Romans 5:1: "Therefore being *justified* by faith, we have peace with God through our Lord Jesus Christ."

Two ideas are expressed in this verse. First, if we are not *justified*, we are at war with God; second, we are to be *justified* by faith through our Lord Jesus Christ.

Paul's words in reverse tell us that because of sin we are not at peace with God. There is a great conflict, or war, going on in this world.

42

God and Satan are at war. Unless we are *justified* we are on Satan's side, fighting against God. Also, God is going to win! See what God's Word tells us about the last great day:

"And the devil that deceived them was cast into the lake of fire and brimstone, where the beast and the false prophet are, and shall be tormented day and night for ever and ever. And whosoever was not found written in the book of life was cast into the lake of fire" (Revelation 20:10, 15).

Death has passed on all of us because of sin. In order to be at peace with God, to be on His side, we must be free of sin. We must be acquitted of our sin and put right with God. We must be *justified*. All right, what does Paul mean —to be *justified*?

In our story, Todd was put right with the law because the judge wanted him to have a chance to make a life without a blot on it. God, our righteous Judge, also wants mankind to have a life without a blot on it. He wants us to be *justified*.

We have established that because of sin we are on Satan's side in the war with God. We want to and need to switch to the other side, but with our sin we cannot escape punishment. We must be acquitted of our guilt, just as Todd was acquitted. Remember that he said, "You mean, Sir, that it's just as if I'd never been involved?" We, too, need to be *justified*: Just-as-if-I'd never sinned. God has made provision for us to reach this position where we "have peace with God through our Lord Jesus Christ. By whom also we have access by faith into this grace wherein we stand, and rejoice in hope of the glory of God. Much more then, being now justified by his blood,

43

we shall be saved from wrath through him" (Romans 5:1, 2, 9).

Only one person in the judge's chambers had the power to put Todd right with the law—the judge who represented the law. Who has the power to put me right (justify) with God? Jesus Christ, who represents God to man and man to God. "The wages [punishment] of sin is death," but Jesus suffered that death, as though He were the criminal, for guilty me. It is just-as-if-I'd never sinned. I am *justified*.

Suppose Todd had told the judge he would return the watch to the rightful owner, help the police to catch the real thief, or do any other restitutional good works. Would this have *justified* Todd? No indeed! The final official decision was made by the judge. He had to say the words that freed Todd. Only when he did this did Todd receive the wonderful gift of freedom.

What makes being *justified* so wonderful? God freely *justified* mankind through the blood of His only begotten Son, Jesus. Man did nothing to earn it. (In fact, there is nothing he *could* do to earn it.) We receive the gift of grace, a free gift that we do not deserve, and are *justified* through our faith in the deed done by Christ, rather than through any deeds we might do: "For when we were yet without strength, in due time Christ died for the ungodly. For scarcely for a righteous man will one die: yet peradventure for a good man some would even dare to die. But God commendeth his love toward us, in that, while we were yet sinners, Christ died for us" (Romans 5:6-8).

Nothing Todd did earned him his freedom. In fact, everything he had done earned him punish-

44

ment. But the judge, because he cared about Todd, took away the blot entirely and gave him the free gift of freedom. It was done on his own terms and his decision was official. Since we are sinners we do not deserve to be *justified*. But God gave Jesus to die for us—for our sins. If we accept Christ's sacrifice, God will extend to us the free gift of pardon. We are then *justified*!

Now, what if Todd did not appreciate his free gift? What if he became involved in another crime? Would he still be right with the law? Of course not! His first actions were not good, but the judge set him right with the law. What Todd does after he leaves the judge's chambers will tell the world and the judge whether Todd wants to continue to be "right" with the law.

What about our *justification*? Paul tells us that after we are *justified* by faith through Jesus Christ, a faith that motivated us to be baptized into Christ as obedient believers, we cannot continue in sin, that is, sin will no longer dominate our lives. "What shall we say then? Shall we continue in sin, that grace may abound? God forbid. How shall we, that are dead to sin, live any longer therein? Know ye not, that so many of us as were baptized into Jesus Christ were baptized into his death? Therefore we are buried with him by baptism into death: that like as Christ was raised up from the dead by the glory of the Father, even so we also should walk in newness of life" (Romans 6:1-4).

The judge did not "wipe the slate clean" so that Todd might go out and help someone steal again, but that he might not suffer punishment for having helped a thief, and that he might not have to live in shame for the blot against him.

So it is with man and God. The life we live after we have been justified tells God and mankind whether we value the free gift of grace. What does it mean to be *justified*? It means, "I know (faith) that God sent His Son to die for my sins while I was not worthy of His grace. I know that I have sinned and am on the wrong side, but I want to change (repentance) to God's side. I know His blood cleanses me of my sins and sets me free. I know this strongly enough that I will tell others (confession) and obey Him in baptism. Then God has made me just-as-if-I'd never sinned (justified) and I can live a new life.

Are you *justified*? Can you say that you have accepted the death of Christ on faith—that His death upon the cross has made you "just-as-if-I'd" never sinned? If not, you and Satan are at war with God, and you are on the losing side. Why not sign your peace treaty with God? "Therefore being *justified* by faith, we have peace with God through our Lord Jesus Christ."

Express Yourself

Since God takes care of our past sins, will He also take care of our future ones? If we need not worry about our past sins, should we be concerned about sinning in the future?

Would it be better to worry about our past sins, and to worry lest we commit sins in the future too?

Is it true that the worse sinner a person was before he became a Christian, the better Christian he will become?

Chapter 7

Love—Won't or Want?

Linda Mackey measured the length of Doctor Parks' desk by letting her eyes move from one stack of papers to the other. It was a large desk. Doctor Parks, sitting very relaxed in his office chair, was also very big. Something about his eyes gave her also a sense of relaxation. It was a good feeling, but now she must speak.

"I don't know, Doctor Parks. When my stepfather comes into the room, I freeze up. I just can't stand him!" She nervously twisted a paper into a tight cylinder. If it had been possible, she would have crawled back into the farthest, darkest, most secret place inside herself so he couldn't see what she was. She didn't love her stepfather, she never had, and she never would! Her fingers twisting the paper grew cold and moist, and the familiar pain in her stomach caused her to wince.

"Linda?"

She looked up, hoping that Doctor Parks couldn't read her thoughts.

"Do you respect your stepfather?"

"Yes, I guess so," she stammered. "I mean— Well, he's fair enough."

"He isn't severe with you?"

"No." She was lucky there. Her best friend, Janie, was often black and blue from her father's discipline.

"Does he make your mother happy?" Doctor Parks persisted.

Linda nodded assent. "It's not that, Doctor Parks. I don't know why, but I just can't love—" she stumbled over the word, "my stepfather. He's good to Mom. She's happy!"

Linda swallowed painfully. It was true. Mom was the happiest she'd been since Dad's accident. The knot grew until pain filled her throat. "He's good to me—I guess. He gives me things. He— Oh, I don't know what's wrong with me!" She put her hands over her face to hide embarrassment for the tears that came.

Doctor Parks didn't say anything for a long time. When the tears stopped, Linda was almost afraid to look up. He probably thought she was terrible, and maybe she was! She didn't want a stepfather—not even to keep Mom happy! She couldn't love him, even if Mom did.

"I can tell you what's wrong with you," Doctor Parks said. A prickle went up Linda's spine. She looked up expecting to see disapproval in his eyes, but his expression hadn't changed.

"You're developing pain because of guilt feelings, and if we don't dissolve those guilt feelings, you'll develop a bad set of ulcers."

"Guilt!" she exclaimed. "You just can't love a person because you want to!" Doctor Parks' eyes probed deeply into her inner hiding place. "And—I guess I honestly don't want to love him."

Doctor Parks shifted in his chair. "I think you do, Linda," he said reassuringly, "but you just don't know how to manage it."

People never agree on *love*. Some feel the world needs more of it; others feel that becoming

48

involved in a romantic or even charitable way sometimes leads to problems, and *love* therefore just isn't worth the effort. Do we have any *love* problems?

Honestly, now, what about our parents? Do we *love* them? Both of them? Equally? Is our *love* problem the kind we read of in Ann Landers' column? Perhaps the problem is the boy or girl sitting beside us right now. Do we really *love* him or her, or will we feel differently next week? Even more serious, our problem involving *love* (or the lack of it) may have begun in a divorce court where our parents ended the marriage that brought us into existence.

Is *love* only a "here today and gone tomorrow" emotion? If it is, how could the beloved apostle John use this word to describe an eternal God: "He that *loveth* not knoweth not God; for God is *love*" (1 John 4:8)?

From the time we were toddlers we may have been taught to *love* God and to *love* others. As we grow older, we find that some forms of love grow into something fine and beautiful while other forms of love do not seem to be lasting. God's Word commands us to *love* one another: "A new commandment I [Jesus] give unto you, That ye *love* one another; as I have *loved* you, that ye also *love* one another" (John 13:34). Furthermore, we are instructed to *love* our enemies: "But I [Jesus] say unto you, *Love* your enemies" (Matthew 5:44). *Come on, now*, some of us may be thinking. *I thought we were being honest! You can't really mean love your enemies.* But Jesus did mean it! In this frame of mind, we have much in common with Linda when she exclaimed, "You just can't love a person because you want

49

to!" And it is here that we begin to determine what *love* really is and what we can and should do about it.

By now we realize that the little word *love* is very broad in scope. Let us take God's Word and analyze the concept of *love* given there. First, we read that God is *love* and therefore our source of *love* (1 John 4:8); second, we know that Jesus said *love* was the characteristic that would show the world that we were His followers (John 13: 35); and, third, we know John stated that if we didn't love our brother whom we have seen, we couldn't love God whom we have not seen (1 John 4:20).

At this point we may be convinced that while *love* is necessary, it is at times next to impossible. We have the same built-up or built-in barriers to love that Linda had, and the effects may be worse for us than the stomach pain Linda felt. Using Doctor Parks' words, we may want to *love* but we "just don't know how to manage it."

In order to manage love for God or man, we must understand the Biblical concept of the word. The language of the New Testament, Greek, has three main verbs meaning "to love": (1) *eran*, sensual love. (2) *philein*, spontaneous, unreasoning affection for friends, homeland, etc.; and (3) *agapan*, the emotion demonstrated in actions, free from the idea of romance or possessing its object. It is the latter of the three, *agapao* (verb form) or *agape* (noun form), that is most commonly translated as *love* in the New Testament Scriptures.

With this in mind, let us ask these questions of ourselves: How do I manage to *love* someone who hurts my feelings, or one who steals from

50

me, puts me in an embarrassing position, lies about me, or gets in the way of something that I want? How do I manage to *love* God who is always invisible and often seems very far away?

Love for God would include the latter two forms of the verb "to love." Most people have no problems involving love for God or Jesus Christ. When a person is first taught about God and the gospel he learns of God's love for him. The apostle John explains this beautifully: "In this was manifested the love of God toward us, because that God sent his only begotten Son into the world, that we might live through him" (1 John 4:9). Also, the familiar verse, John 3:16: "For God so loved the world, that he gave his only begotten Son, that whosoever believeth in him should not perish, but have everlasting life." Further, we know the greatest commandments are "Love the Lord thy God with all thy heart, and with all thy soul, and with all thy mind," and "thy neighbour as thyself" (Matthew 22:37, 39). However, our love is prompted by God's: "We love him, because he first loved us" (1 John 4: 19). As our relationship with God becomes closer, and as our appreciation grows for what He has done, still does, and will do for us, our love for Him becomes deeper.

But this also we must remember: *love* is not merely an emotion; it leads to action. Therefore, in order to *love*, I must act a certain way. All right, how do I act? Determining this is hard, perhaps, but Jesus gave us valuable instructions in John 14:15, 21: "If ye *love* me, keep my commandments . . . He that hath my commandments, and keepeth them, he it is that *loveth* me: and he that loveth me shall be loved of my Father, and I

51

will love him, and will manifest [show] myself to him."

How do we *love* God? We discipline ourselves and behave a certain way to please Him. We do the things He has instructed us in His Word. To know what these things are we study His Word. We worship Him, talk to Him, serve Him, witness for Him. But we cannot forget about our relationship with other people. John plainly tells us, "If a man say, I love God, and hateth his brother, he is a liar" (1 John 4:20). So we cannot ignore people, some of whom we dislike, and some who seem to hate us. How do we love them?

Paul the apostle wrote an unconditionally guaranteed set of instructions for people who want to *love*. Turn to 1 Corinthians 13:4-8, and substitute the word "love" where the passage reads "charity." These instructions can be used on friends or enemies successfully, but for the sake of illustration let us envision a boxing ring with ourselves in one corner and our worst enemy in the other. The bell rings and we come out of our corners. He fights with hate, but we counter with *love*.

"Love suffereth long, and is kind." (This is where we get smacked right on the nose and don't hit back!)

"Love envieth not." (So what if his trunks are fancier than ours and his physique more handsome?)

"Love vaunteth not itself, is not puffed up." (Between rounds we don't show the crowd our biceps, nor demand all the attention.)

"Doth not behave itself unseemly." (We are courteous and kind even when he isn't.)

52

"Seeketh not her own." (We are not out for ourselves alone. Maybe he needs to win this round!)

"Is not easily provoked." (We can take a low blow without giving one back.)

"Thinketh no evil." (We do not add up those bruises and insults and try to figure how to pay back double, but forget them.)

"Rejoiceth not in iniquity." (No punches below the belt, no stepping on toes, no loaded gloves, no gloating over our opponent's injuries.)

"Rejoiceth in the truth." (We fight fairly and honestly, following the rules all the way.)

"Beareth all things, believeth all things, endureth all things." (We can take it as long as necessary; we keep the rules and choose to believe our opponent does; we expect the best man to win; we wait for and accept the referee's decision.)

Our unconditional guarantee is "Love never faileth." Just as surely as hate begets hate, so love begets love. You can overcome an enemy with kindness, or, as Paul says, "overcome evil with good." Try this sometime: pray for that individual you "just can't stand" or who has actually hurt you. People are not perfect, and so our dealings with each other cannot be. Our reactions, though, can be improved if not perfected.

This takes practice. There's a popular saying, "Practice makes perfect," and perfection has a reward! "Herein is our love made perfect, that we may have boldness in the day of judgment: because as he is, so are we in this world. There is no fear in love; but perfect love casteth out fear: because fear hath torment. He that feareth is not made perfect in love" (1 John 4:17, 18).

Do we want to be winners in the game of *love*?

Of course we do! And we can *love* even our enemies because love is not merely an emotion, but a matter of will. Let us remember to practice love, for practice makes perfect, and "perfect love casteth out fear."

Express Yourself

Is it possible to love someone you don't like? Can a person *make* himself love someone?

Should we be in love with ourselves?

How can a person learn to love God, instead of being afraid of Him?

Are there any situations where love will not work?

Chapter 8

Peace Marcher or Peacemaker?

Klaus Straushauer watched his young American friend, Judy Humphrey, change from a chattering teen to a dreamy young co-ed. She had simply walked over and flipped the channel button on the television set, and, as if by magic, she became different. She settled herself into the corner of the couch, drew her feet up under her, and sat with one cheek caressing her shoulder. All of this occurred because a young male singer was crooning a stirring ballad as his fingers moved restlessly over the strings of his guitar.

It is the same everywhere, Klaus was thinking. *In Germany, or in America, young girls react exactly the same way to ballads sung by young men.*

"Isn't he groovy, Klaus?" she asked as the last throbbing note ended the program.

"If you find him so, Judy, he is groovy."

Judy grinned and mimicked him as she said, "I find him so, Klaus. By the way, you're groovy too. I'm so glad Randy brought you home for spring vacation. You're the best surprise yet!"

Klaus found it hard not to be embarrassed by the frank admiration of American college girls, but he had to acknowledge that he enjoyed it.

"I'm glad to be in your home," he answered.

"Want a Coke?" she asked. "Something to eat? I'm starved."

He rose to follow her into the kitchen. As they returned to the family room, wild shouting ripped through the quietness of the pleasant room. From the television set a reporter's voice followed with controlled excitement the action of a student riot:

"Ladies and gentlemen, we are on the campus of Abernathy State College where crowds of students are protesting the war effort. Police battle to keep the protesters contained in the area around Sigmund Hall—"

"Look at the signs, Klaus. 'Peace in Vietnam.' They're surely demonstrating peace all right."

Klaus watched the noisy demonstrators hurling accusations as they pushed and shoved against the police.

"It's so sad," he mused. "All over the world it is the same. Everyone shouts, 'Peace! Peace!' but no one is at peace."

"I know," she replied. Her voice was troubled as she continued. "It makes you wonder what's the matter. How are we ever going to solve the problems? Partly, I feel they're right." Nodding her head toward the demonstrators, she added, "You know, there's not much sense growing up just to be killed over there. But the protesters have such a crazy way of saying it!" She hunched her shoulders as if to shrug off the burden. "Oh, well, at least they're in there, behind the screen, and we're here. And that means," she flipped the channel, "we can turn them off anytime!"

What is the subject of greatest interest to young men today? Perhaps the typical dad might answer, "Girls!" But we would have to suggest another item—the draft. Secretly or openly, young people are weighing the tensions of today against the hope for *peace*, seeking to determine if there can be a future for them. After all, they reason, what do girls mean to the GI lying dead in the jungle of Vietnam?

Peace is an ideal in everyone's heart. Advertisements recruit members for the Peace Corps; newspapers blaze the details of progress or delays in the endless peace talks; scientists explore peaceful uses for atomic energy. *Peace!* Where is it? What is the answer?

The definition of *peace* is not difficult. It means, simply, completeness or wholeness within oneself, and unity or harmony with others. But the application of the principle to life is another matter. Perhaps, like Judy, we may feel there are so many problems that we'll never solve them all. But by reducing statistics to one person, we can each ask ourselves, "Am I at war, or at *peace*?"

"Therefore being justified by faith, we have *peace* with God through our Lord Jesus Christ." By reverse logic, Romans 5:1 implies that man, unless justified by faith in Jesus Christ, is at war with God. So, without faith in Christ, the peace marcher, and the protester of war carrying signs for *peace* is actually at war! *Peace*, then, begins within the person. Wholeness or completeness— *peace*—is accomplished by faith in the justifying work of Christ, because "it pleased the Father that in him should all fulness dwell; and, having made *peace* through the blood of his cross, by him to reconcile all things unto himself; by him, I say, whether they be things in earth, or things in heaven. And you, that were sometime alienated and enemies in your mind by wicked works, yet now hath he reconciled in the body of his flesh

57

through death, to present you holy and unblameable and unreproveable in his sight [justification]: if ye continue in the faith grounded and settled, and be not moved away from the hope of the gospel, which ye have heard" (Colossians 1: 19-23).

If *peace* comes through faith in Christ, then, the medium to that faith is the gospel of Christ. Paul tells the church at Rome this very fact:

"And how shall they preach, except they be sent? as it is written, How beautiful are the feet of them that preach the gospel of *peace*, and bring glad tidings of good things!" (Romans 10:15).

In order for demonstrators, such as those Judy and Klaus were watching on television, to be at *peace* or to achieve the *peace* they desire, they must first be at peace with God. Thinking of the problem of *peace* in this light, it is possible that the GI lying dead in the jungle of Vietnam may have died in *peace*, although he was fighting a bloody war.

"That's a fine thing!" Someone may say. "His *peace* within didn't do much for the *peace* without! Can't we expect any *peace* on earth and find some way to have it?"

His question would really be this: Shouldn't inner peace affect our outer actions? A good question! The Scriptures offer some answers:

"Let us [speaking to Christians] therefore follow after the things which make for *peace*, and things wherewith one may edify [build up] another" (Romans 14:19).

"Follow *peace* with all men, and holiness, without which no man shall see the Lord" (Hebrews 12:14).

58

Yes, peace within should affect our actions. It should cause us to become *peace*makers, and how can we better achieve peacemaking than this—that we carry the gospel of peace to other men?

It is important to keep in mind the fact that man at *peace* with God is at war with Satan. Jesus told His followers that, as a result of the gospel, war would come even between people as close as mother and daughter. Those who reject Christ are at war with God and with all the saints of God: "Think not that I am come to send *peace* on earth: [a strange statement for the Prince of Peace!] I came not to send *peace*, but a sword. For I am come to set a man at variance against his father, and the daughter against her mother, and the daughter in law against her mother in law. . . . He that loveth father or mother more than me is not worthy of me: and he that loveth son or daughter more than me is not worthy of me. And he that taketh not his cross, and followeth after me, is not worthy of me" (Matthew 10:34, 35, 37, 38).

The follower of Christ—a man at *peace* with God—is often at war with his fellowman because of Satan. How is it possible, then, for us to promote peace on earth? Shall we simply endeavor to be at peace with God ourselves, and, as for the rest of the world, say with Judy: "We can turn them off anytime"? No, we can't really "turn them off," can we? Behind the televised picture lay the real "in-the-flesh" incident that will affect Judy indirectly. What, then, can we do about war? The answer lies in being *peacemakers* more than *peace marchers*. The old adage, "Fight fire with fire," has a measure of truth for the Christian. He seeks to overcome man's war with God by

59

waging war with Satan, and this means spreading the gospel of peace to men.

How about each of us? Are we peacemakers or peace marchers? We can be both if we are Christian soldiers "marching as to war"!

Express Yourself

Is it true that no one took notice of the rights of minorities or made significant efforts to end the draft, until massive demonstrations forced the establishment to take notice?

Is violence ever justified to attain a noble goal? If you answered no, what about the American Revolution?

What are some specific ways in which you can work for peace within the climate of today's world?

Chapter 9

Predestinated to an Inheritance

Dru Campbell could almost feel the velvety blackness of the night surrounding her and Scott. It was a dreamy, intimate blackness cut into corridors by swathes of moonlight pouring through the trees and turning the lawn into a blue-white carpet. As they walked, the comfort of Scott's arm draped around her shoulders made the night complete for Dru. No one in the whole world made her feel as complete as did Scott.

"You heard about Gramp's will?" she asked. As she spoke, a familiar sense of frustration crept into her thoughts.

"Yes," Scott answered. "It's great, isn't it?"

"Great?" Her tone betrayed her dismay. "It's just awful! And you think it's great?"

He squeezed her shoulders a little. "Well, I guess so! Thirty thousand dollars is no small sum. I'm surprised that you bother to look at me."

"But there are strings attached," she said. "You know that if I get married before I finish college the money goes to an orphanage!" It made her angry to think about the will. It would be a long, long time before she finished college. Scott would probably marry someone else, and would be lost to her forever! She would never desire to marry anyone else! "Why did he have to do that, Scott?"

"I guess he wanted to be sure you didn't throw away this good chance to complete your education."

"Well, he can't be sure," she replied stubbornly. "I can get married anytime I want to. It's my life!"

"It's your life, but Gramp's money," Scott added, "and he decided on what terms the money could be yours."

"That's right," she said, drawing away from Scott's arm. "Gramp's decided for me that I have to go to college, and that I can't get married when I choose."

There was an awkward silence.

"That's not really fair, Dru," Scott spoke finally. He reached out and gently touched her cheek. "Gramp didn't really decide anything for you. He simply set up the rules. Marry before you complete college, no inheritance; stay single until you finish, thirty thousand dollars. Actually, it's your decision."

Dru closed her hand over his, pressing it against her cheek. It *was* up to her, at that. There was excitement in this moment. Scott, the moonlight, and a thirty-thousand-dollar inheritance were all twisted in kaleidoscopic confusion. It was up to her to make the pieces fall into place.

Let's be honest. Aren't we all just waiting for the day when our Mister or Miss Wonderful speaks those magic three little words: "I love you"? Are any other words as important? Well, there are two other very little words that are extremely important in our lives: "either" and "or." These two words presented Dru Campbell

62

with two different life choices. Standing at the point in life where she is with Scott, she could point herself down "either" one way of life "or" the other. Let's leave her there looking down two separate ways while we begin to examine the Scriptural concept of *predestination*.

Does it shock you a little to learn that *predestinate* is a term found in the New Testament? "Why, the Christian church does not teach *predestination*," you're probably ready to say. But it does! The term is used in God's Word, and Christians accept and believe God's Word! Right here is the evidence: "Blessed be the God and Father of our Lord Jesus Christ, who hath blessed us with all spiritual blessings in heavenly places in Christ: according as he hath chosen us in him before the foundation of the world, that we should be holy and without blame before him in love: having *predestinated* us unto the adoption of children by Jesus Christ to himself, according to the good pleasure of his will. To the praise of the glory of his grace, wherein he hath made us accepted in the beloved" (Ephesians 1:3-6).

"Having made known unto us the mystery of his will, according to his good pleasure which he hath purposed in himself: that in the dispensation of the fulness of times he might gather together in one all things in Christ, both which are in heaven, and which are on earth; even in him: in whom also we have obtained an inheritance, being *predestinated* according to the purpose of him who worketh all things after the counsel of his own will: that we should be to the praise of his glory, who first trusted in Christ" (Ephesians 1:9-12).

"And we know that all things work together for good to them that love God, to them who are the called according to his purpose. For whom he did foreknow, he also did *predestinate* to be conformed to the image of his Son, that he might be the firstborn among many brethren. Moreover whom he did *predestinate,* them he also called: and whom he called, them he also justified: and whom he justified, them he also glorified. What shall we then say to these things? If God be for us, who can be against us? He that spared not his own Son, but delivered him up for us all, how shall he not with him also freely give us all things?" (Romans 8:28-32).

In these passages we are confronted with the word *predestinate*. But how can we say with one breath that we have a choice of "either/or," and with the next say that God *predestinates* us? This is the point where we must separate the Biblical concept from the prelearned misconception of the term.

Predestination is most commonly believed to be a predetermined life for every individual, a life that the individual cannot change, because he was "destined" by God to be good or bad, saved or lost, saint or sinner. If you happen to be one of the lucky ones, good enough! If you aren't, there is nothing you or anyone else can do. Is this the concept that God's Word teaches? If we accept this concept, we must do something about these Bible verses that seem to contradict it:

"The Lord is not slack concerning his promise [to return again], as some men count slackness; but is longsuffering to us-ward, not willing that any should perish, but that all should come to repentance" (2 Peter 3:9).

"For God so loved the world, that he gave his only begotten Son, that whosoever believeth in

64

him should not perish, but have everlasting life"
(John 3:16).

Let us go back to where Dru Campbell stands
facing her decision of "either/or." Could any
part of her life situation teach us something about
the term *predestinate*? Dru does have a choice,
doesn't she? As she said, "It's my life!" But look
again. There is something in her situation about
which she does not have a choice: the end result
of her actions. Scott summed it all up beautifully
when he said, "It's your life, but Gramp's money."
Looking down the two possible avenues of Dru's
life, we can see two possible ends, "either" an
inheritance, "or" no inheritance. And, as Scott
added, "Gramp didn't really decide anything"
for her. He simply set up the rules.

Put yourself before two separate avenues of
life (which is where we all find ourselves) and
put a reward at the end of those two avenues:
salvation for one, condemnation for the other.
You have the choice of the avenue, but God has
predestinated what awaits you at the end of it. In
the same way God has *predestinated*, or chosen
from the beginning, those who trust in Christ "to
salvation through sanctification [we know this
means to make holy] of the Spirit [when we receive Him] and belief of the truth" (2 Thessalonians 2:13). On the other hand He has
predestinated that "they all might be damned who
believed not the truth, but had pleasure in unrighteousness" (2 Thessalonians 2:12).

Gramp determined how Dru could obtain the
inheritance. He knew in advance that Dru would
perhaps be tempted to marry young and forgo
an education, and so he set the terms of His will.
God also knows that each of us will face the

65

decision of walking in righteousness or unrighteousness. He has the inheritance for those of us who walk in righteousness, "Having *predestinated* us [all who believe and trust in Christ] unto the adoption of children [we are His children when we accept Christ] by Jesus Christ to himself, according to the good pleasure of his will" (Ephesians 1:5).

Even though Gramp set stiff terms, he wanted his granddaughter to have an inheritance, and God wants us to have our inheritance in Christ. It is the "good pleasure of His will" that we should have it.

Yes, God does *predestinate*. He has *predestinated* you to an inheritance, salvation in Christ Jesus, if you have accepted Him. He has *predestinated* you to condemnation if you have rejected Christ. Remember, it is your life, but God's terms of inheritance and destination. It is up to you to make the pieces fall into place.

Express Yourself

Considering that I had no choice of my heredity and environment, can I be blamed for what kind of person I turn out to be?

Since God knew that Judas would betray Jesus, do you think Judas was actually carrying out the will of God?

Do you think God has a plan for your life? Can you ever know if He does? If he does, how would you possibly know?

Chapter 10

"Right" Righteousness

Bryan Scott watched enviously as Nick Johnson walked out of the classroom. Nick's departure during the test period meant that he had finished his test paper, while Bryan still had half a page of questions to answer. Only ten minutes left, not enough time to complete the paper. Question four bugged him. What *was* the answer? They had discussed this very question in class only last week. His mind couldn't settle on the remaining questions. He should have reviewed last night, but Carrie insisted on seeing that movie, and what Carrie wanted Carrie got, one way or the other! Lately, she'd been too friendly with Nick.

Nick! Bryan scowled. Bad enough that the guy looked like a superstar, but to have rich parents and brains too—

Bryan closed his eyes and tried to concentrate. As he opened them again, he saw a thin, leather notepad in the aisle between his desk and Nick's. Typical of all Nick owned, the notepad was engraved with his name in silver: *Nick Adam Johnson*. What would someone like Nick write in such a notepad? Carrie's phone number? Five minutes left in the class period! Bryan casually stretched his legs as if they were cramped, felt the pad beneath his foot, and cautiously edged it toward him. Glancing up to be sure he wasn't being watched, he let one hand fall to his side and reached down to retrieve the notepad. *Thornburg looking?* No, he was reading something there at his desk. Bryan thumbed open the pad, and saw that the answers to the test questions were carefully written on the pages. *What was the answer to the fourth question?* Bryan quickly snapped the pad shut without looking up the answer he needed. *No. Play it cool.*

"Mr. Thornburg?" Bryan laid his test paper and the notepad on the desk before the professor. "Nick dropped this as he left the room a few minutes ago."

Mr. Thornburg looked up, nodded pleasantly, and took Bryan's paper, patting the leather notepad Bryan had laid before him.

"Thank you, Mr. Scott," he said. "I'll see that Mr. Johnson gets his notepad."

Bryan smiled as he walked out of the room. Mr. Thornburg would surely look inside. Well, so what? Nick shouldn't have cheated. Thornburg probably would have found it anyway. It was possible that he wouldn't even look inside, but what if he did? Why should he, Bryan, feel guilty? If he wanted to do the right thing, he couldn't cover up for a cheater.

Everyone is concerned with the rightness or wrongness of his actions and the actions of others. We easily recognize that there is a right and a wrong, but sometimes it is hard to make a decision in a particular case. For example, Johnny may see some candy bars in the supermarket and simply put one into his pocket. Another boy sees this and does the same thing. At neither time is the action right, but circumstances may affect our decision. One of the boys may be retarded and therefore not responsible; one of the boys may never have been taught that stealing is wrong; or one of the boys may be so hungry and poor that he cannot resist. Circumstances have a way of preventing "pat" answers.

Honesty demands that we also recognize that some right actions are done for wrong reasons; therefore, right is not always right. Into this confused heap of reasoning let us dump a very difficult word, *righteousness*, and see what we can learn from it.

Do you identify with *righteousness*? If not, you should, for we all are expected to seek *righteousness*. Jesus said, "Seek ye first the kingdom of God, and his *righteousness*; and all these things shall be added unto you" (Matthew 6:33). The apostle Paul wrote a personal letter to Timothy, saying, "Flee also youthful lusts: but follow *righteousness*, faith, charity, peace, with them that call on the Lord out of a pure heart" (2 Timothy 2:22). *Righteousness* must be important, then, but until we determine what *righteousness* is, it is impossible to make it a guide for our lives. Does *righteousness* mean doing right things? We are inclined to accept this definition, but it lacks something vital. Doing right things does not necessarily make the person *righteous*.

Do you really agree with Bryan's reasoning as he gave the notepad to the professor? He really did do the right thing, didn't he? He kept himself from cheating, and this was right. It was right to return the lost property. Was he *righteous*? How did you feel about him?

What was Bryan thinking as he left the room? *Thornburg would surely look inside. Well, so what?* Bryan hoped he would; then Nick would be in trouble with the instructor and probably with Carrie.

What has this to do with *righteousness*? Just this: *Righteousness* means "rightness, justice," as translated from the Greek. *Righteousness*, then, is really *right*ness in our relationship with God and others. While right actions are not always *righteousness, righteousness* makes our actions right. Jesus pointed this out to His followers when He said, "Except your *righteousness* shall exceed the *righteousness* of the scribes and Pharisees, ye shall in no case enter into the kingdom of heaven" (Matthew 5:20). In other words, had the Jewish leaders observed the letter of the law as they claimed, this still would not have guaranteed *righteousness* even to them! Consider Bryan: his action was right, but his reason for the action was so wrong we almost feel that the rightness of his action was nullified. His primary concern was that a rival be taken out of the picture. He used Nick's cheating to elevate himself.

Merely doing the right thing didn't do much for Bryan, and living by the law wasn't enough for the scribes and Pharisees; yet *righteousness* is still so important that Jesus said we must seek it *first*, before any of our other needs. Where do we find it, and how do we get it?

The apostle Paul writes: "The *righteousness* of God without the law is manifested . . . even the *righteousness* of God which is by faith of Jesus Christ unto all and upon all them that believe . . . being justified freely by his grace through the redemption that is in Jesus Christ" (Romans 3:21, 22, 24). Here we find *righteousness* in Christ, and we get it through faith in Him. All right, suppose we have faith in Christ and accept Him as our Saviour. Is this it? Are we now *righteous*?

We know that in God's sight no man is righteous, because of sin. But because God loves us He sent His own Son to the cross to die for our sins. When someone, through faith and obedience, accepts Christ's sacrifice, God considers the person righteous. This does not mean that the person *is* righteous but God *considers* him so. The Christian is in a right relationship with God. He is a "new creature" in Christ. He rises from the baptismal waters to walk in newness of life with his Lord.

But even the Christian finds that Satan still dogs his steps, tempting him to sin, just as jealousy and revenge got the better of Bryan, even after he overcame the temptation to cheat. *Righteousness* must still be sought. Where does the Christian look for it? The Bible, God's Word, is our instructor in righteousness. The Christian must grow in grace and knowledge of the Lord. Paul wrote to Timothy: "All scripture is given by inspiration of God, and is profitable for doctrine, for reproof, for correction, for instruction in *righteousness*" (2 Timothy 3:16, 17). The apostle John also writes, "Whoso keepeth his word, in him verily is the love of God perfected: hereby know we that we are in him. He that saith he abideth in him ought himself also so to walk, even as he walked" (1 John 2:5, 6). The Bible gives us our only example of a *righteous* person: Christ. It is His righteousness we seek. To "walk as He walked" we must read and study His life and teachings, then try to live His example.

By doing these things we can become *like*

Christ, or Christlike; but, even though our attitudes, desires, and intentions may be of the highest spiritual quality, we never do reach the place where we can say in all truth and sincerity, "I am *righteous."*

What do we do, then, give up? What is the use, if all our efforts are in vain? Paul asks this question himself and answers it this way: "How shall we, that are dead to sin, live any longer therein? Knowing this, that our old man is crucified with him [Christ], that the body of sin might be destroyed, that henceforth we should not serve sin. What fruit had ye then in those things whereof ye are now ashamed [the things we wanted to be saved from]? . . . But now being made free from sin, and become servants to God, ye have your fruit unto holiness, and the end everlasting life" (Romans 6:2, 6, 21, 22). What is the "fruit unto holiness"? Some of it is goodness cultivated within ourselves: "Love, joy, peace, longsuffering, gentleness, goodness, faith, meekness, temperance" (Galatians 5:22 23). Some of it is fruit that we present to God, that is, service, so that other souls may be won to Christ. But how can this be done without the other? In other words, if becoming a Christian does not change my life, improve it, make me a better person, how can I convince someone else that this is what Christianity accomplishes?

What have we done to our definition of *righteousness*? It is not only doing the right thing, or what is right according to the law. It is doing what is right in the light of what Christ did and taught, and what His apostles did and taught. "Right" *righteousness* is tempering, or "toning down," the strictly lawful or legal act with mercy, kindness, compassion, after Christ's example.

How important is *righteousness*? How important is your heart to your body? Your life depends upon that little muscle the size of your fist, doesn't it? The Heart Association today stresses the importance of proper rest and diet as protection of the heart, for an increased life expectancy. The apostle Paul stresses the importance of protecting the "spiritual heart" of the Christian. Describing a soldier of his day dressed in armor, he draws a comparison between him and the Christian preparing for battle against Satan. Where does Paul place *righteousness* in this picture? "Stand therefore, having your loins girt about with truth, and having on the breastplate of *righteousness*" (Ephesians 6:14). *Righteousness* protects the heart of the Christian. It has everything to do with our hope of eternal life. We must be found in Christ when He comes again. And, as John tells us, "Every man that hath this hope in him purifieth himself, even as he is pure" (1 John 3:3).

Express Yourself

Do you think it is possible for a Christian to be "too good"? Should we try to be "Holy Joe's"?

Aren't intentions a whole lot more important than outward show? Do the ones who *think* right have a better chance of going to heaven than those who *do* right?

How good do you have to be before God will let you into His heaven? Do you think you will ever make it?

73

Chapter 11

Sacrifice of Service

Mary Wheeler's eyes stopped at the big printed word in the ad section she was reading: "SACRI-FICE: Must sell Smith Corona manual typewriter used six months. Cost $225; will sell for $100 cash."

How long would it take me to repay Mom if I borrowed fifty dollars today? Mary wondered. *It'd be great to have it in my new summer job. Typing college term papers would be simple with a new machine after fighting them out on Dad's old typewriter.*

"Hello, Mary." The cheery greeting came to Mary's ears despite the hum of voices that filled the snack shop. She looked up into the pleasant face of the new youth minister, Ken Felger.

"Hello, Ken," she replied, moving over to let him sit beside her in the booth. "How about lending me fifty dollars? I've found a nearly new typewriter in the ads, and I could use it."

"It can't be very new," Ken said, "if it sells for only fifty dollars."

"Oh, the price is actually one hundred dollars, but I have fifty dollars in savings. The ad says, 'Smith Corona manual typewriter used six months.' See? It says, 'sacrifice.' "

Ken read the ad Mary pointed out to him. He nodded thoughtfully. "Speaking of sacrifices, you made quite a sacrifice yourself, a few days ago."

Mary smiled briefly as she sipped her soft drink. "You mean because of Anne Marie?"

"That's right," Ken answered. "You could have really suffered for your actions."

"What could I do?" she asked. "Anne was heading for serious trouble. Someone had to help her, and I was the only one who knew she was selling marijuana for her father."

Ken nodded. "I know. Chief Jannis said it would have taken the police a long time to get the evidence they needed against Mr. Shefler if you had not helped to set him up for arrest. Not many girls would have done that—for anyone."

"Someone had to help her," Mary repeated. "It is hard to imagine a man using his own daughter for such a rotten business!" Her voice deepened with emotion. "I just pray that we can reach her for Christ, Ken. Helping the police catch that man was a pleasure. It wasn't a sacrifice, believe me!"

"I disagree," Ken said emphatically. "You offered Anne Marie your friendship, and you cared enough to take steps to prove it." He smiled fondly at Mary. "It was a sacrifice, all right, the kind that pleases God."

In the story above, the word *sacrifice* is used in different ways. In the ad Mary was reading, the *sacrifice* was obviously a "sales pitch" from a person desperate for money and willing to take a price below the market value for an article. When Ken called Mary's act of courage a *sacrifice*, she may have disagreed because the word suggested for her a willingness to do something that one really does not want to do. Since we

76

recognize that certain words create several mental images, it is well to consider *sacrifice* and its meaning as used in God's Word. Don't we generally think *sacrifice* means "to give up" something? Actually, the Greek word, *thusia*, translated as "sacrifice" in the New Testament, means "to offer." With this in mind, we'll explore Ken's meaning as he spoke of a *sacrifice* pleasing to God.

The concept of *sacrifice* was first presented in the Old Testament and developed in the New Testament. We could compare the two Testaments by likening the Old Testament to a photographic negative, and the New Testament to the developed print. From Leviticus we get a good outline of the Jewish rites of sacrifice under the law of Moses. In the New Testament we learn of the one great sacrifice to which all the sacrifices of the law pointed. The New Testament presents us also with clear teaching about the kind of sacrifices we are to make as Christians.

Leviticus presents three categories of sacrifice: (1) sin, guilt, or trespass sacrifice; (2) burnt sacrifice; and (3) peace or thanksgiving sacrifice. Also keep in mind that what is recorded in this book may be regarded as a negative of the completed print recorded in the New Testament.

SIN, GUILT, OR TRESPASS SACRIFICE:

Leviticus 4 gives specific instructions for offering this sacrifice. Notice that these instructions were inclusive of all groups. First, it speaks to Israel and its priests: "And the Lord spake unto Moses, saying, Speak unto the children of Israel, saying, If a soul shall sin through ignorance against any of the commandments of the Lord concerning things which ought not to be done, and shall do against any of them: if the priest that is anointed do sin according to the sin of the people; then let him bring for his sin, which he hath sinned, a young bullock without blemish unto the Lord for a sin offering" (vv. 1-3).

Specific instructions for carrying out this sacrifice are given in the next nine verses, then there is a provision for the whole congregation: "And if the whole congregation of Israel sin through ignorance, and the thing be hid from the eyes of the assembly, and they have done somewhat against any of the commandments of the Lord concerning things which should not be done, and are guilty; when the sin, which they have sinned against it, is known, then the congregation shall offer a young bullock for the sin, and bring him before the tabernacle of the congregation" (vv. 13, 14).

Next it speaks to the ruler who has sinned: "When a ruler hath sinned, and done somewhat through ignorance against any of the commandments of the Lord his God concerning things which should not be done, and is guilty; or if his sin, wherein he hath sinned, come to his knowledge; he shall bring his offering" (vv. 22, 23).

Finally, this chapter mentions the common people (ARV translates this phrase as "people of the land"): "And if any one of the common people sin through ignorance, while he doeth somewhat against any of the commandments of the Lord concerning things which ought not to be done, and be guilty; or if his sin, which he hath sinned, come to his knowledge . . ." (vv. 27, 28).

Thus Leviticus points out that *all* had sinned

78

and needed a *sacrifice* to offer for that sin. The New Testament contains the same evidence. The apostle Paul writes, "For all have sinned, and come short of the glory of God" (Romans 3:23). Customs, cultures, and civilizations may change, but human nature apart from God never changes. Man sins. Because of that sin, which is an offense to God, he needs a *sacrifice* to offer God.

Leviticus gives the acceptable *sacrifice* for sin and the method for offering it. Who, then, is to offer the sacrifice for our sins? Who is our high priest? What sacrifice is to be offered? The answers to these questions are found in the letter to the Hebrews: "But Christ being come an high priest of good things to come, by a greater and more perfect tabernacle, not made with hands, that is to say, not of this building; neither by the blood of goats and calves, but by his own blood he entered in once into the holy place, having obtained eternal redemption for us. For if the blood of bulls and of goats, and the ashes of an heifer sprinkling the unclean, sanctifieth to the purifying of the flesh: how much more shall the blood of Christ, who through the eternal Spirit offered himself without spot to God, purge your conscience from dead works to serve the living God?" (Hebrews 9:11-14; read also Hebrews 10:19-22). As sinners we need an offering or *sacrifice* for our sins and we need a high priest to offer it for us. Our *sacrifice* and our high priest are one and the same, Christ Jesus, who offered His own body and blood as a sacrifice for us and took it into heaven itself to offer it to God.

Man sinned, making the sacrifice necessary; otherwise man had no part in the sin offering. It was done for him by a high priest. The New

Testament underscores this fact that man can do nothing to remove his sin. It has been done for him. He must simply accept the sacrifice.

This is one concept of *sacrifice,* but is it the one that Ken referred to in his discussion with Mary? No. Since it isn't, let us check the other two kinds of *sacrifice.*

BURNT SACRIFICE:

Leviticus outlines the burnt offering in this manner: "And the Lord called unto Moses, and spake unto him out of the tabernacle of the congregation, saying, Speak unto the children of Israel, and say unto them, If any man of you bring an offering unto the Lord, ye shall bring your offering of the cattle, even of the herd, and of the flock. If his offering be a burnt sacrifice of the herd, let him offer a male without blemish: he shall offer it of his own voluntary will at the door of the tabernacle of the congregation before the Lord" (Leviticus 1:1-3). Notice the words, "He shall offer it of his own voluntary will." The burnt offering differed from the sin offering in that it was a voluntary act symbolizing the worshiper's complete surrender to God. Turning now to the New Testament, let us examine the developed picture of the burnt offering concept: "I beseech you therefore, brethren, by the mercies of God, that ye present your bodies a living sacrifice, holy, acceptable unto God, which is your reasonable service" (Romans 12:1). Paul is speaking of a "voluntary will" sacrifice in which the person offers his daily life as a sacrifice to God.

Looking back to the story of Mary Wheeler, remember that Ken said, "You offered your friendship and you cared enough to take steps to prove it." Mary was involved. Her love for God and for her classmate prompted her to offer herself in service, or a living *sacrifice*. As Ken said, her *sacrifice* was pleasing to God. There are many ways of demonstrating this type of sacrifice to God. Consider, for example, Philippians 4:18: "But I have all, and abound: I am full, having received of Epaphroditus the things which were sent from you, an odour of a sweet smell, a *sacrifice* acceptable, well pleasing to God." This indicates that offering our material wealth for the service of God can be a voluntary act of personal surrender. Our "burnt offering" can be any sacrificial act that we do of our own free will in an effort to demonstrate before God our surrender to Him.

PEACE OR THANKSGIVING SACRIFICE:

"And if his oblation be a sacrifice of peace offering, if he offer it of the herd; whether it be a male or female, he shall offer it without blemish before the Lord. And he shall lay his hand upon the head of his offering, and kill it" (Leviticus 3:1, 2).

The peace or thanksgiving *sacrifice* was a voluntary sacrifice and was shared with God. Comparing this type of sacrifice with the New Testament, we note the following exhortation in the book of Hebrews: "By him [Christ] therefore let us offer the *sacrifice* of praise to God continually, that is, the fruit of our lips giving thanks to his name" (Hebrews 13:15). Our praise to God offered in the name of Jesus Christ is the New Testament concept of the peace or thanksgiving offering. We are involved. We share the offering with God when we worship Him because of Christ.

81

Thinking back to Ken and Mary, the picture becomes clearer. Because of their mutual fellowship in the local church, Ken knew that Mary had acknowledged the *sacrifice* of Jesus for her sins when she had accepted Him. Christ, her high priest, had offered His own body and blood as a sin *sacrifice* for Mary Wheeler. Ken knew that Mary offered the *sacrifice* of praise and thanksgiving to God. Because of her actions on behalf of Anne Marie, Ken interpreted her life, and her desire to win Anne Marie for Christ, as a "living *sacrifice*."

How about each of us? Have we accepted the offering of Christ as our sin sacrifice to God? If so, are we offering the daily sacrifice of a life lived to God through service to others? Do we offer the sacrifice of praise and thanksgiving in communion with God without expecting our parents, the church, or the minister to offer this sacrifice for us? If we can answer yes to these questions, we have something in common with Mary Wheeler. We are offering *sacrifices* that are pleasing to God!

Express Yourself

Does sacrifice mean giving up something we would like to keep, in order to give it to God? Do we really sacrifice if it has not hurt? If we enjoy doing or giving it, can it still be a sacrifice?

Is it proper to sacrifice something to God in order to get the reward He has promised?

Chapter 12

Soiled or Sanctified?

Jean put her hand gently over Tim's and pulled it away from her knee. With a deft movement she took his other hand, brought both of them forward, and clasped them between her own.

"This isn't for us, Tim. We're forgetting who we are."

Tim's dark head moved closer to her own and his very nearness started a trembling inside her.

"Jeannie!" he pleaded.

"No, Tim." She pulled herself away from him, crowding against the door until the handle bit into her ribs.

"I'm sorry, Jean," Tim said gruffly. "I didn't mean to let things get out of hand."

"It was my fault, too, Tim. We'd almost forgotten who we were."

Tim reached out a hand to ruffle her hair. "You, Jean—me, Tim," he bantered in an effort to lighten the gravity of the situation.

"No, Tim. We're Christ's." She caught his hand again and squeezed it.

"I know," he answered. His voice dropped to a whispered prayer. "Thank God, we are His—tonight!"

He turned the key in the ignition and, as the motor roared to life, switched on the lights and slowly pulled back onto the highway.

Shall we look inward for a minute? Put yourself inside one of the characters in this story,
Jean or Tim. If this had been your story, would
it have had the same ending? Whether you are a
Christian or not, the same physical urges and
temptations trouble you. Surprisingly enough,
being young has little to do with that. The problem
seldom decreases with age, only the circumstances.
What made the difference with Tim and Jean?
Was it because Jean wasn't tempted? No. Remember that his nearness started a trembling
within her. She wanted to give in to her natural
urges. What made the difference? The fact that
they were Christians made them recognize temptation, but what really made the difference was
that they were Christians who had learned to live
sanctified lives.

Let us take a long look at that long word
sanctification. What pops into your mind when
you see this word? Perhaps you see it as a religious idea, having something to do with saints,
either living or dead. Aside from the Scriptural
use, it is not a word used in daily vocabulary,
but it is a word with which every Christian should
be familiar, and it is an attribute that every Christian should have. Webster's dictionary defines it
as *to make holy, to make free from sin, to set
apart as holy* or *to consecrate*. As applied to a
person it means *to make holy*, or *to make produc-
tive of spiritual blessing*.

Young's Analytical Concordance of the Bible
gives the Greek word *hagiasmos* for our word
sanctified, meaning to separate, or set apart. The
word for *holy* is also *hagios*, translated to separate, set apart. Used in 1 Peter 1:16, "It is
written, Be ye holy [hagios]; for I am holy."

We can determine, then, that *sanctification* is synonymous with holiness. *Sanctification* is a spiritual concept, generally thought of in connection with saints. But we are mistaken if we think a saint is a being on a higher spiritual plateau than that of Christians. According to the New Testament, all Christians are saints. Our term *sanctification*, or holiness, applies to every Christian. You may be thinking, "Holy? Me?" But let us examine the Scriptures carefully before we rule this out.

Apart from Christ, man was and is unholy, a sinner separated from God. Once a year the old Jewish Day of Atonement was observed, with the blood of animals atoning for the sins of the people during that year. Israel was *sanctified* (made holy) by the blood of bulls and goats offered by the high priest that one day in the year.

"But into the second [Holy of Holies] went the high priest alone once every year, not without blood, which he offered for himself, and for the errors of the people . . . For if the blood of bulls and of goats, and the ashes of an heifer sprinkling the unclean, *sanctifieth* to the purifying of the flesh—" (Hebrews 9:7, 13).

The old covenant (old will, law) was for the Jew, and its provision was not for all time. The Christian is under the new covenant (new will). How is he *sanctified*? How were Jean and Tim sanctified?

"Then said he [Jesus], Lo, I come to do thy will, O God. He taketh away the first [old covenant, law], that he may establish the second. By the which will we are *sanctified* through the offering of the body of Jesus Christ once for all. And every priest standeth daily ministering and offering oftentimes the same sacrifices, which can never take away sins: but this man [Jesus], after he had offered one sacrifice for sins for ever, sat down on the right hand of God . . . For by one offering he hath perfected for ever them that are *sanctified*" (Hebrews 10:9-12, 14).

How does a person become *sanctified*? Only through the blood sacrifice of Jesus Christ. We could never stand before God as holy, without the blood of His Son covering the sins of our lives. The remission of sins is gained through the shedding of His blood. "And without shedding of blood is no remission" (Hebrews 9:22).

Now, if you are baptized for the remission of your sins (Acts 2:38), can you take a deep breath and say, "That's settled. Now I am holy"? If God through the blood of Jesus Christ *sanctifies* me, is there anything further for me to be concerned about? God has lifted me out of my sinful state and placed me in a new state of *sanctification*, or holiness. For the sake of a mental picture, think of this "state" as my being on a kind of pedestal. All right, here I am where God has placed me. Do I have anything to worry about? Only one thing: Satan. Satan will continually try to get me down from that pedestal so that he can claim me. Oh, he won't be so obvious as to push or pull me off. He will be very subtle, using my weaknesses and desires, and so entice me to climb down of my own accord. Consider Jean and Tim. Did they need to be concerned? Indeed they did! Satan tempted them, and their temptation could have led to a real situation with a less happy ending. How can we, real, living characters be assured that we can overcome our temptations, and stay where God has placed us?

86

God knew that His people would have difficulty living holy lives as long as Satan was working, and yet He demanded holiness. Is God unreasonable? We know better. God always makes provision for our needs. He has promised that He will not allow us to be tempted above what we are able to stand. Also, with the temptation He will provide a way of escape so that we can overcome it (1 Corinthians 10:13). Jesus promised the Holy Spirit to comfort and guide us (John 14:16). In praying for us that we might be *sanctified*, He named the source from which we can get the help needed to live *sanctified* lives:

"I pray not that thou [God] shouldest take them out of the world, but that thou shouldest keep them from the evil. *Sanctify* them through thy truth: thy word is truth" (John 17:15, 17). God's Word, then, helps us. It continues the process of our sanctification. From it we learn to conduct our lives in holiness.

"Furthermore then we beseech you, brethren, and exhort you by the Lord Jesus, that as ye have received of us how ye ought to walk and to please God, so ye would abound more and more. For ye know what commandments we gave you by the Lord Jesus. For this is the will of God, even your *sanctification*, that ye should abstain from fornication [sexual relations before marriage]: that every one of you should know how to possess his vessel in *sanctification* and honour" (1 Thessalonians 4:1-4).

"What? Know ye not that your body is the temple of the Holy Ghost which is in you, which ye have of God, and ye are not your own? For ye are bought with a price [Christ's blood]: therefore glorify God in your body, and in your spirit, which are God's" (1 Corinthians 6:19, 20).

If you are a Christian, you are involved in *sanctification.* Your will determines whether or not God can use your life and body for good works. Paul wrote these words to Timothy, whom he loved dearly: "Let every one that nameth the name of Christ depart from iniquity [sin]. If a man therefore purge himself from these, he shall be a vessel unto honour, *sanctified,* and meet for the master's use, and prepared unto every good work" (2 Timothy 2:19, 21).

Yes, you are involved in your *sanctification.* Do you want to be used of God for good works? Consider this idea:

No one ever pours clean, pure water into a dirty glass and offers it to a thirsty person. Neither will God pour the water of life from a soiled vessel to refresh a thirsty sinner. Do you want God to use your life? It is important, then, to be like Jean and Tim, to remember who you are. You are a Christian, you belong to Christ, and you are *sanctified.*

Express Yourself

Do Christians participate in holding hands? Necking? Petting? Sexual intercourse with one's fiancée? Intercourse with a steady? With anyone? Where would you draw the line, if at all?

Criticize or defend this statement: What we do when we are together is our business, and does not involve anyone but ourselves.

If sex outside of marriage is so bad, what is in the marriage ceremony that changes things?

Chapter 13

What a Fellowship

A cold drizzle settled against Greg DuBarry's cheeks. With numb fingers he wiped the moisture from his eyes, leaving a muddy trace against his nose. Beads gathered on his eyelashes and forehead. Under his heavy shoulder pads the muscles of his back twitched. This was it! The final minutes of the football game, and State was only one point behind. There was still time.

Suddenly the play was on—the snap, the fake, and the long arching pass. Against a leaden sky the football sped straight and sure to Greg. He braced himself for the impact, raised his arms slightly to receive, and there it was, solid and sure in his arms. Then the muddy missile became alive. It twisted in his grasp and flew out. Greg lunged toward it just as another pair of shoulders made their way into his path. He was down and gasping for air until pain made breathing impossible.

"Hey, fella!"

Greg opened his eyes reluctantly to the sound of Jim's voice. It was Jim Matthews, who had sent the ball soaring in his direction.

"Jim!" Greg answered. His chest was gripped with a hot band of pain.

"Hold it, Greg. No talking! You're a little busted up." Jim put his hand awkwardly on the covers of the hospital bed.

"We lost our chance for championship," Greg grunted through tight lips, "because I fumbled the ball."

"Forget it," Jim said. "The game should have been called because of field conditions. I'm just sorry you're in that sack."

"Oh, come on!" Greg exclaimed. "I lost the game for State. Why hide it?"

"*We* lost the game," Jim replied pointedly. "No one plays the game alone."

Greg lay looking quietly at Jim for a minute. "So you're going to have your share of the game, no matter what, is that it?" He managed a weak grin. "Do you like being a loser?"

Jim grinned back and rubbed a hand reflectively over his chin. "Seems I remember a score that made us winners. Let's see. It was a week ago, wasn't it?"

It was true. Last week they had been winners all the way. "But I didn't fumble last week," Greg protested.

"Win or lose," Jim said, plopping into the chair by the bed, "we're a team, and don't you forget it!"

Exactly what is meant by the term, "Christian *fellowship*"? We sing the old hymn, "What a fellowship, what a joy divine," but do we know what it means? Turning our mental eye inward, let's get a picture of what we "see" when this word *fellowship* is mentioned.

Picture a long table covered with all kinds of delicious foods, and church friends talking and laughing as they fill their plates. Is this the picture that *fellowship* brings to our minds? Perhaps some of us would be more likely to envision this scene: We are in someone's living room with all the kids from the youth group. There is laughing and talking as we play games, and in the kitchen we hear the rattle of dishes as someone prepares refreshments for the party. Is this the *fellowship* of the church?

Let's decide first whether or not the term *fellowship* should be used by the church, and if so, how it should be interpreted. The beginning of the church is described in the book of Acts, so that is where we should find a clue to how the early church interpreted the word.

"Then they that gladly received his word were baptized: and the same day there were added unto them about three thousand souls. And they continued stedfastly in the apostles' doctrine and *fellowship*, and in breaking of bread, and in prayers" (Acts 2:41, 42).

It would seem from this Scripture that *fellowship* was linked equally with doctrine in importance in the early church.

"That's good," some may say. "Let's have more church potlucks (with Mrs. Smith's chocolate cake) and lots of youth parties. *Fellowship*, that's what we need!" But shouldn't we establish first what *fellowship* really is according to the Bible? For example, try to connect the Scripture below with the above concept of *fellowship*: "That I may know him, and the power of his resurrection, and the *fellowship* of his sufferings, being made conformable unto his death" (Philippians 3:10).

These words of Paul obviously have no reference to a social or party. Something must have happened to the word or to our thinking. How

91

did people begin to limit the concept of *fellowship*, generally speaking, to the social activities of the church? And what did Paul mean by "the *fellowship* of his sufferings"?

The meaning of a word often changes through the years, and confusion results in the mental picture that the word produces. Some of us may have had some explaining to do the first time we told our mother that she looked "tough." And, do our parents really dig the phrase, "sock it to me"? Why do they react as they do? Isn't it because the mental picture the word creates is different from ours? Time has changed the meaning for us.

In order to understand the New Testament writer's words, we must examine the picture drawn by the New Testament language. The Greek word, *koinonia,* which is translated as *fellowship* in the New Testament, meant "partnership; sharing in common; sharing partnership." Let us go back to Philippians 3:10 and check out what Paul was really saying: "That I may know him, and the power of his resurrection, and the *fellowship* [sharing partnership] of his sufferings, being made conformable unto his death." Paul was saying that he desired a sharing partnership in the sufferings of Christ.

Shall we step back into the hospital room where Greg lies in a bed? Greg is suffering physically from his injury, but he is obviously suffering mentally as well. Isn't it true that we often hurt worse from humiliation than from bruises? Yet Jim was willing to share Greg's humiliation. As a team member he said that *all* were winners, or *all* were losers. They shared the outcome. Just as the whole team shared a previous victory, now they shared defeat.

Now, as we look at the Scriptures again and think of what Paul meant when he spoke of the *fellowship* of Christ's sufferings, we recall that the cross was not only an instrument of great physical torture, but a source of deep humiliation for the person who hung there. Note what Paul had written earlier in Philippians concerning Christ and the cross: "And being found in fashion as a man, he humbled himself, and became obedient unto death, even the death of the cross" (Philippians 2:8).

God's own Son, sinless and innocent, sharing our physical form, died a painful and humiliating death when He could have commanded the hosts of heaven to protect Him. As a servant of Jesus Christ, Paul had willingly shared the same kinds of suffering his Master had endured. He had been subjected to physical distress in many forms and he had also undergone the bitter experience of humiliation.

To a lesser degree we also share Christ's sufferings in this way. We may not have been beaten or openly persecuted for our faith, but many who have been faithful in their Christian witness have at least known some uncomfortable moments of rejection or ridicule by those they have tried to win. In any case, the Christian pledges loyalty to Christ. He will remain faithful whatever trials he may have to endure.

Paul taught that *fellowship* means sharing in common, not only our relationship with Jesus Christ, but also material things, "Praying us [Paul and Timothy] with much intreaty that we would receive the gift [money collected by the churches of Macedonia for the poor saints at Jerusalem], and take upon us the *fellowship* [sharing partnership] of the ministering to the saints" (2 Corinthians 8:4).

We are taught that we have a sharing partnership in the gospel as well. "I thank my God upon every remembrance of you, always in every prayer of mine for you all making request with joy, for your *fellowship* in the gospel from the first day until now" (Philippians 1:3-5).

As immersed believers in Christ, we also are sharing partners of the Holy Spirit. "If there is therefore any exhortation in Christ, if any consolation of love, if any *fellowship* of the Spirit, if any tender mercies and compassions, make full my joy, that ye be of the same mind, having the same love, being of one accord, of one mind" (Philippians 2:1, 2, American Standard Version).

What is the *fellowship* of the church? The beloved apostle John gives details for the relationship that draws all men into one sharing partnership: "That which we [the apostles] have seen and heard declare we unto you, that ye also may have *fellowship* with us: and truly our *fellowship* is with the Father, and with his Son Jesus Christ" (1 John 1:3).

Consider what our feelings about God might be right now if He had never sent Christ. This was real *fellowship*! He shared His Son with us, but better yet, Christ *shared* our common lot with us. He experienced the physical and emotional needs common to us, and He faced and overcame *our* world's problems. We have fellowship with God through Christ.

There is also a fellowship of victory still to come. Jesus Christ already experienced this, rising victorious over death and ascending to the right hand of the Father. He "for the joy that was before him endured the cross, despising the shame, and is set down at the right hand of the throne of God" (Hebrews 12:2). This victory is also ours through Him.

Can we now see *fellowship* in a larger dimension? Can we see ourselves, all the apostles, our Christian ancestors, our present Christian family members, and even our unborn children who will accept Christ, all on the same team, all involved in a real sharing partnership that bridges the generation gap from creation to eternity? If we do, it is with good reason that we sing, "What a *fellowship*"!

Express Yourself

Who is your Christian brother? Will there likely be anyone in heaven with whom you would not fellowship and work together here on earth?

How important is it to keep yourself away from those who are not living according to the will of God?

If we take Jesus as our example, how will we relate to those who we feel may not be living according to God's will?